Copyright © 2009 by Regina C. Anderson and Betty Glover Palmer
First Printing 2009

Printed in the United States of America

Library of Congress Cataloging-Publication Data

Published by:
Sisters On The Journey, Inc.
1101 Cascade Park Drive
Atlanta, Georgia 30331
404-344-3419

Cover and Interior Design by Lessie Matthews

ISBN978-0-615-31678-9 (soft cover)

For copyright information and additional copies contact:

Betty Glover Palmer, Managing Editor
4472 Hunters Way
Stone Mountain, GA 30083
404-299-0041
Email: sistersonthejourney@yahoo.com

Blessings To you!

Dr. Regena C. Anderson

Sisters On The Journey
Their Songs ~ Their Stories ~ Their Transformations

Rev. Dr. Regina C. Anderson, Editor

Published by: Sisters On The Journey, Inc.

Prologue

"....Yet who knows whether you have come to the kingdom for such a time as this?" ~ Esther 4:14

About Sisters On The Journey, Inc.

Little did I know when I was baptized at the young age of six that God was calling me to my destiny of ministry to Sisters on the Journey. I was an only child – no biological brothers or sisters – but spiritually I had sisters among my church and Christian community. Across the years and the miles, we bonded together in a unique way, and I seemed to be the un-appointed leader of the group.

I can remember vividly my first activities with this group of teenage girls called the "Sunbeam." The song, "Jesus Wants Me for a Sunbeam" was our motto and theme. It was not very long before we, the little Sunbeam group, became an official church ministry – a young "Sisters on the Journey," so to speak. God blessed the sisterhood to span across the country, i.e. Las Vegas, Maryland, Washington, D.C., Texas and California. To this date, we have not strayed from prayerfully connecting as Sisters on the Journey via letters, phone calls and visits.

After many years, I was ordained and licensed as a minister. My calling to Christian Education and Counseling entrenched and made plain my supportive role to women and their relationships. The linkage between the original Sunbeams and my ministry to women expanded and embraced women across the country. God had destined many of us to relocate to Atlanta, Georgia and we were able to offer support, solace and encouragement to each other. Caring, sharing and empowering one another fertilized the future ministry group that now exists with its base in Atlanta, Georgia. In 1996, I founded Sisters on The Journey, along with other dear sisters, Edna Hartwell, Libby West and Llona Speede. Our spiritual connection superseded ages, occupations, denominations and our individual journeys.

i

About "Sisters On The Journey Book"

This book shares many of our life stories and many are told through Negro spirituals. Because of the richness of these sisters' lives, I was inspired to have us write our stories. Stories were gathered from across the nation and across generational lines and cultures. Stories are grouped into seven themes: The Journey Begins, When the Road is Rough, Journeying On, Transition to Purpose, You Shall Live and Not Die, Abundant Life Realized, and Praise God from Whom All Blessings Flow. We hope sharing our collection of journeys will be a blessing to all who read it. You are welcome to join us on the journey.

We now have more than 30 "Sisters on the Journey" who connect and live a life of "caring, sharing and empowering." No one ever needs to feel disconnected or alone because we have each other. No matter where we go – the north, the east, the south, the west – we are there to share and care for one another. Our regular meetings address our spiritual and social needs with prayer, Bible study, book discussions, social activities and encouragement through our successes and failures.

I am grateful to our Sister On The Journey, Rev. Betty Palmer, who has been the managing editor and driving force, charting our course and leading us to this mountain top experience. Her faithfulness, organizational skills and countless hours and labor have ushered us into a new level of sisterhood that spans miles and embraces generations.

Rev. Dr. Regina C. Anderson, Founder and Editor
Sisters on the Journey, Inc.
A Ministry of Caring, Sharing and Empowering

Foreword

One of the most memorable dialogues in the movie version of Alice Walker's novel, "The Color Purple," is a scene that takes place between Miss Celie (Whoopie Goldberg) and her abusive husband (Danny Glover) known simply as "Mr."

When Celie, after years of abuse, decides to stand and declares her independence and resolve to leave her abuser, Mr. yells, "Look at you, you're black, you're poor, you're ugly, you're a woman, you're nothing at all!"

Miss Celie, now emboldened by life's experiences, shouts back, "I'm poor, black, I might even be ugly, but dear God, I'm here." After all she had endured, she was able to declare by the grace of God, "I'm still here."

Sisters On The Journey is an inspired collection of testimonies written by women who have faced and endured some of life's greatest challenges and are able to declare, by the grace of God, "I made it through." Wow, how inspiring!

Sisters on the Journey is a timely word of encouragement and hope for both women AND men regardless of their age, circumstance or situation in life. For this collection of testimonies reminds each of us that all of life is a journey, a journey that can be treacherous, tough, confusing and at times, heartbreaking. These writings remind us that the journey of life is often thwarted with uncertainty, confusion and indecision which can easily produce a sense of powerlessness that feeds negative emotions. Sometimes it's easier to focus on the negative, drown out the beauty that is abundant all around us, disappear inward and ultimately lose sight of whose we are and who we are. Too often situations in life appear insurmountable and the easiest thing to do is give up.

But the testimonies of these incredible women encourage all of us to not give up. Their testimonies are a reminder that God is still God and He is still able to do abundantly more than we can ever ask, think or imagine.

iii

Sisters On The Journey encourages us to focus on the beauty around us, live in the moment, know that whatever pain we may experience on the journey enables us to grow as individuals; enables us to develop a deeper understanding of who we are; enables us to rediscover that God is leading and guiding us and will bring us to His preferred future for our lives.

As you read this book, the experiences of these women will encourage and remind you to hold on and not give up or as the writer of Hebrews says in Hebrews 10:23-25, "Let us hold firmly to the hope we profess, for He who promised is faithful.

And let us consider how we can spur one another on towards love and good deeds. Let us not give up meeting together, as some are in the habit of doing, but let us encourage one another – and all the more as you see the day approaching."

Through *Sisters On The Journey*, Dr. Regina Anderson and her *Sisters On The Journey* have inspired and encouraged each of us to hold on and not give up. Thank you, Dr. Anderson, and all you "sistahs" for sharing your journey with us.

Rev. Dennis Mitchell, Senior Pastor
Greenforest Community Baptist Church
Decatur, Georgia

About the Editor

Rev. Dr. Regina Anderson

I am unable to pay Dr. Regina Anderson the huge debt that I owe her, her daughter Joy, and the love of her life, the late Clayton Anderson for their heavy investments in my career and in the lives of the large J. Alfred Smith clan. From the very beginning of my Allen Temple pastoral ministry, Regina and family were present with countless creative suggestions for molding the membership into a loving family. She helped me bring widely, nationally known speakers to the church and spent many hours cooking exquisite and palatable Louisiana cuisine which all of us ate in their spacious home. No hostess was more gracious than her daughter Joy. Regina set the record as Business and Professional Women's President in raising $50,000 for scholarships for high school graduates and continuing college students. No one to this day has exceeded her amount.

Regina, as a professional educator, established the Hi-Rise Tutorial Program at Allen Temple Baptist Church, which for some 38 years, continues to elevate the academic performance of middle school and high school students in the areas of math and science. Other churches have adopted the Hi-Rise Tutorial model, which brought the public schools into a close Allen Temple partnership. Regina also brought parent participation to a new level in the Oakland Schools.

Dr. Regina Anderson is a group harmonizer. She galvanizes individuals into happy, productive groups. She has held the Allen Temple clan, who now live in Georgia, into a loving group. My pastoral short sightedness failed to organize, from her efforts, Allen Temple East in Georgia. How true it is that hindsight is better than foresight. Again, she is the founder of a Christian para-church ministry – Sisters On The Journey, a ministry of caring, sharing and empowering Christian women.

Regina C. Anderson is a retired educator from Oakland, California and a Christian Educator from Atlanta, Georgia. She was an adjunct professor in Christian Education at American Baptist Seminary of the West and lecturer, religion consultant and mentor of countless young ministers. She has one daughter, Joy L. Coffey, a school counselor in Atlanta, Georgia.

It gives me great pleasure in saluting the accomplishment of Dr. Anderson's book. She has earned the right to produce a helpful book like this work. But most of all, I must put in writing my deepest gratitude to her.

Read her words. Meditate upon them. Share this book as a gift to others.

Prayerfully,

J. Alfred Smith, Sr.
Senior Pastor, Allen Temple Baptist Church

Acknowledgements

Producing this book, *Sisters On The Journey*, has been an incredible piece of work that exemplifies both the love and labor of many sisters. This book is a project of Sisters on the Journey, Inc., a ministry of sharing, caring and empowering. Our fearless leader and founder of Sisters On The Journey, Rev. Dr. Regina Anderson, planted the seed more than five years ago, affirming that all of us had a story worthy of sharing. The seed was constantly watered and now God has given the increase!

I had the wonderful pleasure of working alongside Sister Regina and others, managing the editorial administrative, and publishing tasks. The many articles came to us in various stages of completion. The untiring editing efforts of our three sisters transformed the articles into a beautiful manuscript. Many thanks to Rev. Patricia Boyd-Wilson, Minister Rhonda Hicks and Yvonne Givens for their expertise and many hours spent in editing and fine-tuning the articles. Pat, Rhonda and Yvonne, you exhibited much patience as we continued to submit articles and relocate articles far past the editorial deadlines. The final editing was done by Elder Alonia Jernigan. We are so thankful for your keen editorial gifts.

The elegant book cover was designed by Lessie H. Matthews who felt our heart and produced this masterpiece.

Gratitude goes to Rev. Paula Stallworth who used her creativity in organizing the articles into thematic groupings. Gratitude is extended to Suzette Geffrard who gave early leadership to the project and oriented us to the writing process. Terrie Brown, thank you for coordinating the marketing and public relation strategies to promote the book. Throughout this entire process, Joy Coffey provided dynamic administrative assistance and organized the articles into a systematic database. Joy, you're the best!

To all forty of my sisters far and near, who wrote and rewrote your article, thank you for sharing your touching stories that will surely be a source of inspiration to our readers.

And to our queen/leader, Dr. Anderson, we are so glad that you were obedient in carrying out God's vision to write this book. All of us sisters who wrote articles have experienced healing and joy.

We thank you for you transformational leadership and inspiration.

To God be the glory for giving us the courage to be transparent and pen these pages!

Betty Glover Palmer
Managing Editor and
Vice President
Sisters on the Journey, Inc.

TABLE OF CONTENTS

x

The Journey Begins

Faith of Our Mothers
Sisters on the Journey – An Allegory
Patricia A. Boyd-Wilson

"...we will tell the next generation the praiseworthy deeds of the LORD, his power, and the wonders he has done...so the next generation would know them, even the children yet to be born, and they in turn would tell their children. Then they would put their trust in God and would not forget his deeds but would keep his commands." ~ Psalm 78:4-7

Once upon a time there was and is a wonderful African queen who lives in a lowly mansion in the great Metro Land. Her demeanor is a mixture of characters from a southern novel and she speaks with the accents of the ancient dark mothers. She is known in many lands as the African Queen Mother and in some circles as a doctor who heals with a mighty touch of words and homemade concoctions from her royal kitchen.

African Queen Mother had a vision unlike any other vision. Her vision rolls on and on like a 3-dimensional, technicolor movie with Surround Sound. Only the Almighty King of Kings can tell you where such a vision came from and where or if it will end. I can tell you that it's Queen Mother's vision and she's got to use it.

She can't be separated from her vision; it's part of her formidable character. As the village storyteller I would like to tell you all that I can about how the vision came to be a part of our lives. Then perhaps you can decide if you want to come to our kingdom to meet the African Queen Mother for yourself.

Several years ago, African Queen Mother summoned all her surrogate daughters to the mansion on computerized parchment prepared by the only royal princess, Joy the Lovely. We were met with the hospitality of the mansion whose doors were like an open smile to everyone. After we were seated, African Queen Mother told us that we were the seeds from which her vision would sprout and grow.

"I see young black peasant 'gr-elles' (her pronunciation of girls) and brown princesses marching like a Nubian army on parade in the capital city," Queen Mother announced without warning. We understood that girls meant women in the prime of their lives. Yet, we were mesmerized by the tone of her voice and the mood of the moment, so no questions were asked about what she had said.

"You must be prepared to journey back through the lands of Knocked Down Island, Back Row County and Criticism City to bring other Nubian peasants and princesses from far and near to our kingdom. Then we can begin training for future journeys and for the wars of life so that everyone can reach the continent of Divine Destiny. Our first step is to recognize our sameness so that we can support one another despite our perceived differences." Queen Mother rose from her seat moving counterclockwise around the circle as if sizing all of us up for the journey.

We were from many different villages and townships; a small but motley crew. Some were from Widows Ville, and others were from Professional Country. Still others were from Bare-foot Homeland and others from Labor Camps inside Metro Land. We gaped at one another trying to find those perceived samenesses that Queen Mother apparently saw. Except for our attachment to Queen Mother, we would never be together anywhere else in the world, at least not on purpose.

"Gr-elles!" She beckoned us to attend to every word as she returned to her seat. "Listen, everything that happens, happens in

3

God's appointed time. The Almighty orders our footsteps and things that we could never plan just unfold right before our eyes. That's why you're all here together at such a time as this. Understand me well, it's all about caring, sharing and empowering one another and others to reach Divine Destiny."

As she spoke, Queen Mother peered over her gold-rimmed spectacles making sure every daughter was captured by her spiritual and visible authority. Princess Joy the Lovely preserved every word on new parchment, recording our names for posterity and position. None of us understood the importance of that moment except the princess who knew the intentionality of her mother better than anyone. Yet, somehow we knew we should treasure each verbal morsel.

"Gr-elles!" She maintained verbal command of the court. "There is a great journey before us and we must make sure no one arrives alone! Everyone must reach back, reach over and reach out! We must use our voices, our talents, our gifts, even our pains and struggles. Yes, we must use our stories to help every sister on the journey arrive at her divine destination in wholeness. Are you listening to me?" She queried with her eyes and her crooked red-tipped index finger.

We were silent, but we were listening. Some nodded; others looked around with moist foreheads and clammy fingers. It was as though we were waiting for a physical manifestation of her words. Finally one brave sister gained the courage or the insight to speak.

"Queen Mother," she ventured, "we, or at least some of us, want to make the journey but we are still nursing our injuries from the former journeys of our younger years."

"You know how hard it was to just get here," another sister chimed support for the first.

"Yeah!" went forth a quiet consensus.

"I don't know who to trust, so how am I going to be trusted to help someone else?" A brown skinned Mary-Kay princess proclaimed.

"I heard that!" said a Maybelline Labor Camper.

"I can't identify with some of these sistahs from the Professional Country," one caramel colored sister from Divorce

4

Township exclaimed. "Once I was on that road, but I lost everything I had and there was no one to help me!"

"That's real," came from the sidelines anonymously. Then a woman from the coastal lands where Queen Mother originated took the floor with boldness.

"We're from everywhere, different parts of the world, different backgrounds and different agendas. We can't be expected to work together, can we?" There was a stir of dismay and resentment among us. If Queen Mother hadn't called us to attention we would have divided into our own little niches or simply wandered away.

"I will speak now!" Queen Mother rose to her bare feet, her golden Kinte stole draped over one shoulder. "This is why I've summoned you here. You have a choice. You can believe the lie that women can't be sisters and soul mates; that we can't trust one another and that we must go the journey alone, but understand it is a lie! We are women, Nubian women, whose heritage and roots give us a commonality that others do not have. We have been heifers, "B's," little sistahs, sweet mammas and a variety of other adjectives. Some of us have been abused, abandoned, raped and discarded while others have been pampered, favored and elevated by class or color. Yet, we've had to prove ourselves by doing our duties one hundred and fifty percent better in our homes, our jobs, our schools and even our churches just to be recognized."

"That's real," the sideline girl sang out again.

Queen Mother strolled across the court; her stature seemed to grow with every step. She spoke softly to make us lean in a little closer.

"We can care for one another; we can empower one another and generations to come. We can support and network and school one another because we are of the same soul, the same dark African fabric, and we can trust the Divine Source of our being to lead us, because He will guide our steps." She touched some of the sisters on their faces and shoulders as she passed by. Tears and smiles beamed across the court because we definitely trusted her. She had been our individual confidante, mentor and nurturer. She was proof of the possibility.

"I know you gr-elle," she spoke to a widow woman and all of us at one time. "I've been there! I have my scars too! I don't like to brandish my wounds, but I have them," she said lowering her royal gown just enough for us to see the healed gash near her heart.

"Ohh!"

"My God!"

"Mother!" Singular sighs and comments seemed to materialize all over the court as she readjusted her regal robes to cover the historic scars from her previous journeys.

"When I say, 'You can get through it,' I know what I'm talking about. And when I say we can bond together I know about that too. The truth is none of us made it this far by ourselves. Some sister, some momma or grand-momma held our hand and paved the way. The journey is not easy and the cost is not cheap, but together we can cover the cost and become the conductor for other women to reach the continent of Destiny." Queen Mother always denied being a preacher but she was preaching an effective sermon to our longing ears.

"I will feed you with the words of authors and sisters who have made the journey before you. We'll enjoy the coastal cuisine with our testimonies and prayers. Queens will come from other countries to encourage and empower us so that we can release the phantoms of our past and the Heavenly Father will order our sister steps until we become a voice and a ministry to be reckoned with." These words evoked silent agreement and thoughtfulness. You could almost see the muse move miraculously across the court as we began to embrace the vision.

Queen Mother did and is doing all these things just like she committed to us individually and collectively. We began to capture and own the vision one by one. We were freed, we were healed, we were inspired and we were sisters active on the journey. We began bringing others to the mansion and repeating Queen Mother's majestic message.

Then one day, we received communication from Princess Joy the Lovely that all should come to the mansion for a new mandate. We arrived with much chatter and excitement prepared to receive the food of wisdom from our dear mother. Queen Mother prayed for all of us and she shared more of the vision with us.

"I don't profess to know the details, but I know your stories and they need to be told. The telling of your stories will help our younger sisters and our aged sisters keep moving on the journey. Your stories are tools, not baggage, for you to carry everywhere you go. It's time to empty those bags, and allow others to learn and become free, become empowered by the victory of your stories. I want you to continue to embrace the vision as it grows from seed to fruit, sharing, caring and empowering every sister as we move to the next level. I want you to write your stories. Then we will distribute them on computerized parchment for sisters everywhere to read and to know that they can reach Destiny too!"

Many of us are trying to be obedient. Many of us have accepted the challenge to journal our testimonies and tell them to another generation. Still, we don't know where this vision will take us or what new mandates will come forth. But we know we're all better for the journey in our togetherness.

Queen Mother's vision is alive. It's not like any other vision. Its ending is far into the future, generations from this telling. I can only tell you what a village storyteller knows. There are many sisters out there and they all have stories to tell. If you look carefully into the eyes and hearts of the women you meet each day, you'll meet a Sister on the Journey, and if you ask and listen carefully, she may tell you her story.

Patricia A. Boyd-Wilson is the senior pastor and founder of Saint Luke Christian Ministries. She is a member of the College of Pastoral Leaders of Austin Presbyterian Theological Seminary and an active member of the Light of the World Interdenominational International Association. She also serves as a public speaker and facilitates many Christian Education venues for women of all ages. Additionally, Pastor Pat is the owner/director of Guided Steps Early Learning Center in Stone Mountain, Georgia.

When The Road Gets Rough

My Soul Looks Back and Wonders
Rev. Dr. Regina C. Anderson

"Blessed are those who mourn, for they will be comforted." ~ Matthew 5:4

My years of training and experiences have taken me on many ministering paths with "those other people." I have actively served as a grief counselor and knew the red flags. I was confident in holding their hands and steadying their feet as they walked through "this season of their lives."

Recently, my daughter's father died. He had returned to the family in Atlanta after being away and remarried for more than 30 years. Because there had not been a recommitment between us, and he had again remarried, I assumed that his dying would be routine and "just another thing." Not so!! I found that I was unable to sleep, had low energy, felt anti-social with a loss of appetite and preferred to be alone. "What is this," I thought. This behavior is not usually displayed by me.

After hours and days of wallowing in my own uncomfortable space, I decided to see my doctor. I explained my rollercoaster feelings to him. He immediately said, "Sounds to me like depression." I resisted his diagnosis but he insisted, as a medical professional would, and recommended that I take medication and see a therapist.

I began to "look into the mirror" and talk to myself. In fact, I became a companion to an empty chair. I began to go back into the recesses of my mind and deal with unfinished issues that I had not brought closure to. I reviewed the high points and low points. It was not only the grief of my former husband, but I began to review and embrace my life's journey. I had stepped over other losses and had not completed the grieving process. The residue from previous losses had accumulated and was now lying dormant, covered up, but simmering, festering and incomplete. I assumed that with a busy nest, I could fill the empty space.

I had lost a son at a very young age, but I assumed that I had to be strong. I busied myself doing things. I worked with many other grievers but I did not work with myself. In fact, it seemed natural to work with others; I took to it very well. I was overlapping or covering up my pain without completing the grieving process. I ignored other losses also; those that had nothing to do with death, like loss of home, neighborhood or relationships. I had moved from California to Atlanta, losing my lifetime friends, church and everything comfortable and familiar.

I remembered the "Grief Wheel" that I used when ministering to grieving families. I remembered how many times I talked about unfinished or overlapping grief. "To participants, it does not just go away," I would often say, "It may take months or even years." Those words came back to me as I remembered the strategy of conversation with an empty chair. Remembering, recalling and talking back to an invisible person sitting in a chair before you may be the road to healing and recovery. Things that are in the recesses of your mind are recalled — maybe pushed down, covered over, yet still there, but incomplete.

If you have unfinished grief, look in the mirror and talk to yourself.

Dr. Regina C. Anderson is a native of New Orleans, Louisiana. She accepted Jesus Christ as her personal savior at a very early age. She was licensed and ordained by Rev. Dr. J. Alfred Smith Sr. Dr. Anderson's educational achievements include: Bachelor of Arts in Education, Dillard

University, New Orleans, Louisiana; Master of Arts in Education, San Francisco State University, San Francisco, California; Master's of Divinity, American Baptist Seminary, Berkeley, California and Doctorate in Ministry United Theological Seminary, Dayton, Ohio. Dr. Anderson is currently residing in Atlanta, Georgia with her daughter.

A'int That Good News
Rhonda S. Hicks

"Lo, children are a heritage of the LORD: and the fruit of the womb is his reward." ~ Psalm 127:3

"Broad-based gait." I will never forget those words, which did not reflect "good news." They were just the beginning of many words that would create for me a journey a bit more challenging than the average mother's.

My baby, due on May 2nd, made his grand entrance into the earth six weeks early. My doctor's attempts to stop his delivery were futile. The neo-natal team stood by in the delivery room ready to whisk my little one off to their area of the hospital. It was not to be. My son weighed in at exactly five pounds and except for a slightly low temperature, was as feisty as any little one could be. The neo-natal team left alone with an empty incubator while my husband stood with his arms filled with our new son.

Christopher was a wonderful baby who nursed aggressively and enjoyed the affections of his brother and sister. He did not lift his head, scoot, roll over or stand as early as his siblings, but the pediatrician assured me that though delayed, "these children usually catch up." As predicted, he did all of those things. In fact, once

Christopher started walking, he was a spirit to be reckoned with. He was a funny fellow who got into everybody's things. He hated the car seat, the stroller and the grocery store cart. He wanted to get down and do his own thing. He was the child who, when we were out, had the baby friendly, colorful "leash" which was intolerable to every African-American I knew. It was either that, so as not to lose my child, or a constant day of bickering. Christopher had his freedom and I my sanity. He sat quiet for meals (even in restaurants), Sunday school and church and whatever REALLY interested him.

By 2-1/2 years old, Christopher was chattering away but his language was unintelligible. While many tried to assure me that it was too early to be concerned, his father was, so we had the pediatrician refer us to specialists. That was when my life, our lives, changed. After much testing, our baby was diagnosed as being developmentally delayed. The doctors recommended physical, occupational and speech therapy. He had a broad-based gait and had to wear braces on his legs at night. It was determined that he had an attention deficit and was hyperactive (I called it curiosity). Medicines were prescribed which I would not allow. God had sent me a very healthy son and those "remedies" were potential hazards to his health. The Holy Spirit and a second medical opinion made it clear that Christopher was not hyperactive after all.

It's been 23 years since those days. Christopher is 25 years old and is a very handsome, articulate and, I must say, interesting young man. He has a well-earned high school diploma. He loves to sing, works with the youth in our church and has a job. Christopher has an amazing sense of humor, has many friends and is a joy in the life of our community. He has been slapped with such labels as Developmentally Delayed, Learning Disabled, and Mildly Intellectually Delayed (MID). He is presently viewed as an "Adult with Disabilities" by the state of Georgia. That not withstanding, he is a child of the King who God both sent and wanted here.

The journey has not been easy. I've had to "battle" with systems, others' opinions, a teen-aged and adult Christopher, and even God. This is a lifelong journey that I don't always want. For me, the terms "empty nest" may not become a reality. I've had to search my soul, repent and change my belief system so that it aligns with God. I've had to humble myself and seek counseling so that I could better parent my child. But, he his mine and most of all, he is God's. "Ain't That Good News"!!

Minister Rhonda S. Hicks is an associate minister of Greenforest Community Baptist Church and is the Bible/Religion coordinator for the Greenforest McCalep Christian Academy, both in Decatur, Georgia. She is married to Clarence Hicks and they have three adult children. Her favorite scripture is Psalm 127.

Somebody Prayed For Me
Joanne Chatman

"Likewise the Spirit also helps our infirmities: for we know not what we should pray for as we ought: but the Spirit itself makes intercession for us with groanings which cannot be uttered." ~ Romans 8:26

Surely somebody prayed for me. At that time, somebody had to be or had been praying for me because I could not pray for myself. My life was going downhill, fast like a rollercoaster ride. Everything I knew had changed. I had gone from being a wife of 21 years to a divorced woman. I had also gone from being a parent and mother of three to being a mother of just one; at least it seemed at that time.

After moving from the place where I had lived for 19 years to an apartment with my youngest child, my daughter, I felt so alone and it appeared that everyone had deserted me. I wanted so much to talk to someone. Instead I lay on the apartment floor on a blanket with my child trying to be brave. I lay there thinking how I got there, wondering how a person who promised to love, cherish and hold me turned into an abuser. I could find no peace, no contentment. I ached, I hurt and I was alone.

Somebody prayed for me. I left my mom's house in Alabama to come to my husband's house in Georgia and I found myself leaving his house to move to my own house. My life at that point was not as I had dreamed. I was experiencing something new and I was afraid – mostly afraid to be alone, though I had been alone for some time even in the midst of being married and with my family. Now I was really alone with a child who was looking to me for comfort. We both were afraid.

Times came when my daughter had to go to her father's house for weekend visits. This was the hardest for me, for then I really was alone. I missed her so much on those weekends. Sometimes I would come home from work and cry all night. During those times I wondered how I was going to get over this pain. I missed everything that had been my life, even though it was not all good. My daughter went to visit her father and brothers, but my youngest son refused to visit me. The oldest one would not talk to me. I was so angry and the pain was almost unbearable. Nothing had prepared me for this, nothing. I blamed the man that I had been married to for 21 years. Somebody prayed for me. Through all of the hurt and pain, somebody had to be praying for me.

There was a time when I would call my friends and I could not find them. I wanted some words of comfort, some words of en-couragement. I wanted someone to just listen, but I found no one. I knew the LORD, but I was trusting people more than Him for my comfort, my peace. Somewhere in the midst of all my pain, my hurt and my tears, Jesus started working on me. He began to soothe my aches, my pains and dry my tears. He began to calm my fears. I remember one weekend when I was alone and trying desperately to find friends to talk to, but I could not find one. That's when I fell on my face and cried out to the Lord for help. I cried out to the LORD and He rescued me. He gave me peace and calm assurance that He would never leave me nor forsake me – that He would always be there. Somebody prayed for me.

Joanne Chatman is a member of the ministerial team at St. Luke Christian Ministries in Stone Mountain, Georgia. She is a graduate of Beulah Heights University and received her B.A. majoring in Biblical Leadership.

Through It All
Jackie Ransom

"There hath no temptation taken you but such as is common to man: but God is faithful, who will not suffer you to be tempted above that ye are able; but will with the temptation also make a way to escape, that ye may be able to bear it." ~ 1 Corinthians 10:13

Everyone has a different journey in life. If someone had told me 21 years ago that I would not be married 20 years later I would have laughed hysterically and even would have bet money they were wrong. I used to question God, myself and often wonder, "Where did everything go awry?" As I have grown spiritually stronger as well as mature, I no longer ask questions such as, "Why me, Lord? Why does my character need to be strengthened?" I simply live each day understanding that His ways are not my ways and His thoughts are not my thoughts.

This particular journey began in May of 1987. I bumped into my future husband while on a weekend visit in Nashville, Tennessee. A man that was one of the most popular people at Tennessee State University pursued me. He was articulate, intelligent and charming with a brilliant mind. The first night we went out, we talked until 5 a.m.! We quickly "fell" in love and were married about 363 days later.

We were the "perfect" couple. We had so much in common. We were both "jocks" and loved all kinds of sports. We had friendly competitions in basketball, tennis, racquetball and bowling -- just to name a few. We were the talk of the town. Life was blissful. We hated to leave each other in the mornings when we had to go to work because we didn't want to be apart for that long! I would never have dreamed that 12 years later I would discover a "crack" pipe in my home. At the time, my ex-husband's nephew stayed with us. Due to my inexperience and lack of exposure to drug paraphernalia, I had to ask the nephew what the pipe was. He simply dropped his head and replied, "Oh man!" Alarmed I asked, "What's wrong?" He stated, "I know he is not on *that* stuff!"

I was in denial about this whole situation for at least six months. It blew my mind and petrified me to think that my knight in shining armour was on drugs! I would wake up in the mornings hoping it was all a nightmare! After experiencing money quickly leaving the bank accounts, his passing out regularly on the sofa and discovering "crack rocks" on his person, I knew I needed help. With the help of my "surrogate" mother, mentor and spiritual advisor, I found a therapist that helped me through this turbulent time in my life. I will always remember her because she guided me through one of the darkest moments in my life. She helped me to grasp what was happening and deal with the reality of what was occurring.

After coming to grips with my situation, I then sought marital counseling. Radical Love was the name of it. Their mantra basically was that your spouse is not "your" problem, you are. In other words, the course takes the approach that each spouse looks introspectively versus outside to identify the problems. It takes two to make a relationship work. I often thought of my marriage vows, "…for better, for worse, for richer or poorer, in sickness and health." My attitude and disposition in life is simple. Give everything you have in all situations so that you never look back and wonder, "Did I do everything I absolutely could have?" I have lived by this mantra, so the day I decided enough was enough, I knew I had given my all.

I attended Narcanon meetings. I prayed. I cried - all the while trying to understand "Why." When a person gets addicted to drugs, they are not the person you once knew! You see the person you knew, but they don't act the same. My husband would have these fits of rage to the point where I was trying to figure out if it was safe to be in his presence.

I experienced so many "crazy" things. My wedding ring and tools from my interior decorator business were pawned. I had my father's drill and found it had been pawned along with a friend's miter saw that was at my house. I got to the point where I felt like a prisoner in my own home! I locked my purse in my van in my garage every night along with my tools and anything else I needed to hide and protect from being pawned. When I went to bed at night I would pray that I would have everything in the morning that I had before I went to bed. I experienced my checkbook being stolen along with my debit cards. I also had my van taken for two days leaving me with no transportation and trying to figure out how long I could deal with and handle this.

One thing is for sure. I look back on this life changing experience and understand that God will never allow you to go through more than you can bear. When you think you are at the edge and you can take no more, He will always "have your back" and give you a way out. A lot of my closest friends and family members often say, "I am glad you finally got out." But nobody can decide how much you can take or bear. We must all live our lives separately and independently. Just because it works for one doesn't mean it is right for the next.

Jackie Ransom is a native of Nashville, Tennessee. She has resided in Atlanta, Georgia since 1986. She attended Vanderbilt University on a full basketball scholarship where she received her B.E. in Electrical and Biomedical Engineering. She is the sole proprietor of Sew Unique Interiors, a full service interior design firm. She also coaches high school girls' basketball at Southwest Atlanta Christian Academy. She is divorced with one 24-year-old son.

Flowers From Mommy
Llona Winifred Speede

"Even to your old age, I am He, and even to gray hairs I will carry you! I have made, and I will bear; even I will carry, and will deliver you." ~ Isaiah 46:4

On Saturday, December 17, 2005, I returned to Goldsboro, North Carolina to visit for the very first time since our Mom was laid to rest. I called my sister Jane when I drove over the bypass into town. She was at Wal-Mart with her daughter Nicole and her friend Sherri and I met them there. When we arrived at the house Sherri looked at me as I pulled up next to the van. She said, "Aunt Llona looks just like Grandma."

Jane later told me, "I really didn't pay her too much mind because she's young, a little silly and I was thinking about getting my groceries into the house." Jane was sitting in the recliner where Mom used to sit when I walked through the door with my weekender bag in hand.

The living room was well lit which gave Jane a chance to get a good look at me. She told me later that she was absolutely startled by what she saw. Jane said she was glad that she was sitting down. She didn't mean to stare at me but she couldn't seem to take her eyes off of me. She told me that I looked just like our mother. I looked at Jane incredulously and said, "No I don't!" A photo of our Mom that was taken over 60 years ago sat on the mantle. I had given Jane a photo of myself two months earlier. I took the photo in hand and walked over to the fireplace. Jane stood by me and I put my photo next to Mommy's. It was then that I saw what Jane saw. It was unmistakable. The resemblance between the two photos, one of Mom and the other of me was startling. Our mother was gone but her energy and spirit were still here with us. Mom's spirit was so evident in Jane's life in the way that she ministered to the children and others in her community. And Jane clearly saw Mom's spirit in my face and in my life as well.

Mom was an amazing woman with an indomitable spirit. She was always "the mother" and Jane and I never forgot that. We are both grown with adult children and grandchildren. However, we were still our mother's children and when she called our names we answered, "Yes Ma'm." When it became apparent that it was no longer safe for Mom to live alone, Jane and her husband, Mr. Wood, made a place for Mom in their home. The transition was smooth and Mom fit right in. She was doted on by everyone in the house. Her room was beautifully decorated. She was surrounded by her precious furniture and things. Family and old friends came to see her and she just loved it. Jane's house became her home. She was the queen and she reigned.

Mom was with Jane for over two years when a lump was discovered above Mom's left breast. Dr. Tabe ordered a biopsy. He called us in two days later to tell us that the results of the test were malignant. Neither Jane, I or Mom panicked. Our quiet peace came from God. Some family members felt that Mom was unaware because of her aging signs. In spite of the evidence of Mom's dementia she was still "Mom" and she fought to hold on to her person. Her long term memory became more prevalent than her short term memory. Mom recalled events and time periods from years past with great clearness of thought. She relished sharing those memories with me and I enjoyed these times immensely. Mommy was the family griot. Her faith was still in tact. She prayed for family, extended family and friends and spoke from her place of God's wisdom when she counseled. There were times when she spoke words that were prophetic. Many realized this months later when the words she spoke came to pass.

When it came to Mom's medical treatment, my other sisters and family members had their own opinions. A sister friend, Dr. Regina, encouraged me to ask my mom what *she* wanted to do about it. I returned to Goldsboro the very next weekend and after dinner I sat with Mom in her room and spoke with her about the lump and the biopsy report. I asked her, "Mom, what do you want? Please tell us what you want us to do."

Mom looked at me with eyes that were fully present. She spoke with a mind that was crystal clear and her words did not falter. She said, "Let them take the lump and I will trust God to do the rest." I called Jane to come and Mom repeated her request for Jane's ears to hear. Unfortunately, my other sister who had the authority to make medical decisions for Mom would not hear or abide by our mother's request.

At the age of 85-years-old, Mommy underwent and survived a radical mastectomy. After a five day hospital stay she was discharged. Jane and I brought her home. We assisted her out of the car and up the stairs (slowly with her walker) to the front door. Jane opened the door and Mom walked across the threshold on her own. As she took those measured but strong steps she said to me, "Sis, be it ever so humble, there's no place like home."

It turned out that Mom's trust in God was not in vain. The additional biopsy report proved that her breast was cancer free. Mom fully recovered from the surgery and reassumed her position as teacher, counselor, standard bearer and Queen in Jane's house / her home. God is excellent in all His ways.

One day Jane returned home from an appointment later than she intended. Mommy was back from the senior center and the children were home from school. Jane found Mom sitting in "her" favorite recliner chair by the fireplace. Jane's seven-year-old grandson, DJ, was sitting at Mommy's feet. As Jane began to prepare the evening meal she asked DJ if he'd studied his spelling words. He told her that he'd studied and that he knew them all. Jane asked, "How did you test yourself?"

DJ replied, "Great-Grandma tested me."

Jane found this hard to believe. Mommy added to her confusion when she said, "DJ did good, he got 100%." As Jane stood there looking bewildered, Mommy pulled the index cards the spelling words were written on out of her house-dress pocket. Then she shared with Jane her method of testing DJ. Mommy gave him each word in a sentence and when he spelled it correctly she checked it off. Jane was even further astounded when she realized that Mommy still remembered the multiplication tables and was using her "house-dress pocket system" to help her great-grandson learn math. Mommy began to help her three great-grandchildren with their homework and had no problem correcting their behavior whenever she felt it was warranted. At the age of 85, Mommy was full of surprises and still full of life.

I committed to drive up every six weeks from Atlanta to spend my weekend with Mom and to help my sister Jane. Mommy loved plants and flowers and I would always bring her a new plant or some flowers whenever I went to see her. This became my "signature" and a "secret reminder" of our special mother - daughter relationship. Christmas of 2004, I drove up to spend my weekend with Mom. I brought her a rosemary bush shaped like a Christmas tree and I decorated it. She absolutely loved it. She sat it next to the beautiful black lighted angel I'd given her that graced her hope chest. I took Mom out for our traditional Christmas drive to see the holiday decorations in the various neighborhoods. I had the CD player loaded with some of her favorite Christmas songs. She sang "Ave Maria" with Barbara Streisand. She sang "Joy to the World" and "The First Noel" with Nat King Cole. She knew every word of the songs she sang and she hummed the melodies of the rest. We "oohed" and "ahhed" at the beautifully decorated homes, laughed and sang all the way back. She told me that she had a wonderful time. Mommy joyfully walked up the steps with her walker and little assistance from me when we got back to Jane's / her home.

Another sister obtained a court order for joint guardianship and in mid January, Mommy was moved from Jane's home against her will. But she was still Mommy and no one was going to boss her around. Thirty four days later on February 20th, Mom went "home." She chose to make her transition before daybreak on that particular Sunday morning. Jane and I were sad in our hearts but we also had the peace of God that surpassed all understanding (Philippians 4:7) because we were the very best daughters to our mother that we could have possibly been. We honored her with all that we had. We gave her "her flowers while she yet lived."

Now we were blessed and comforted by our beautiful Mommy-memories and our sisterhood. And if that was not enough, within two weeks after Mom went home, Jane's front yard was filled overnight with brilliant yellow daffodils.

It was too early for daffodils to come up. It was still cold outside but we felt the warmth of Mommy's love every time we looked at all of the barren front yards as far as the eye could see and then looked at a hundred or more yellow daffodils in bloom before us, right outside of Jane's front door. The daffodils come up in Jane's front yard every year, early in February. It has become Mommy's "signature" and a sweet reminder to us of the special mother-daughter relationships, the love that she held for us and other family members who loved, cared for her and shared those beautiful times with her there. God is indeed excellent in all of His ways.

Llona Winifred Speede was born in New York City, the eldest daughter and second eldest of eight children born to St. Clair E. Speede and Gertrude J. Speede. Llona has a B.A. in Biblical Studies, is a licensed and ordained minister, and has conducted relationship workshops for teens and adults in Colorado and Georgia, high schools, universities and churches spanning 20 years. She continues her ministry serving as director of the After School Program at Greenforest-McCalep Christian Academy, ministering to students, their families and the community at large.

Journeying On

I Loved Him Through It
Cynthia R. Rolle

"Wives, likewise, be submissive to your own husbands, that even if some do not obey the word, they, without a word, may be won by the conduct of their wives, when they observe your chaste conduct accompanied by fear." ~ 1 Peter 3:1-2

This is the story of how the agape love of God saved my marriage. I had come to the place where I had become weary and was ready to give up on my husband because of his alcohol and drug addiction. It was destroying our marriage.

On the morning of September 28, 1996, I was ordained as a minister of the gospel, and on the afternoon of that same day, I was married to my beloved husband whom I had known for 15 years. He shared with me later that he remembered me from elementary school, junior high and high school. I didn't realize that we had attended the same schools. I met my husband at our 10-year high school reunion. I admired him because he was a brilliant and successful young man with his own business. He was a master electrician who eventually became an electrical contractor, which led him to millionaire status. What he *didn't* share with me was that he had an addiction to alcohol and drugs.

He hid the addictions very well because he was a functional

alcoholic and drug addict until his business began to fail. He began to drink even more and eventually began to stay out late at night without calling me. I knew something was wrong and that alcohol was not his only problem. As I continued to pray for my husband, he seemed to get worse and stayed out later and later. Occasionally, he wouldn't get home until the next morning and then his time away from home turned into days, sometimes as many as two or three without calling. He finally admitted that he was addicted to drugs, but that his biggest problem was alcohol.

My first focus was on myself and what I was going through with this man whom I thought I knew. Here I was, a minister of the gospel with a husband who was an alcoholic and drug addict. I became weary and began to lose hope. I admitted to God that I would be happy with Jesus alone and was willing and ready to divorce this man that I had asked God for.

My husband had given his life to Christ so he was saved, but he wasn't delivered. I was convinced that I wasn't strong enough to take his behavior any more. Therefore, I ran to the church for help. We were attending World Changers Church International where there was a substance abuse ministry in place to help people like us. I told my husband about it and encouraged him to attend with me. He refused to go the first time but I went anyway because I was at my lowest point and I needed help.

The substance abuse ministry didn't give me a pity party when I shared my situation with them. After allowing me to share, they identified my problem as co-dependency. They didn't speak about my husband's addiction, but they gave me love and instruction in the Word of God that dealt with what *I* was going through. The Word of God was like a mirror, which caused me to examine myself. All I wanted them to tell me was that it was all right for me to divorce my husband. I was tired of praying for him and wanted out of the marriage. However, what I received was the love of God, the Word of God, and prayer. After the one-hour meeting was over we were directed to the church for Bible study taught by Pastor Creflo Dollar. Bible study was a mandatory requirement of the substance abuse ministry. Seats had been reserved for us and we all worshipped together.

While driving home, the Holy Spirit spoke to me and said, "Don't give up on your husband; I didn't give up on you." I heard those words clearly within my spirit and I knew that the Lord was speaking to my heart. I love God more than anything or anyone, including my husband, and I truly desired to please Him. When He spoke to my heart, I spoke back to Him, and cried out to Him and said, "Father, if you want me to stay with my husband, you've got to do something because I'm weary, and you said that you wouldn't put more on me than I could bear. I can't bear it anymore."

I shared with my husband my experience at the substance abuse ministry and assured him that it wasn't like Alcoholics or Narcotics Anonymous where they confess that they are alcoholics and drug addicts. They had us to confess that we were overcomers, and that we were overcome by the blood of the Lamb and the word of our testimony. My husband began to attend the meetings with me and received the love of God, the Word of God and prayer. After my husband expressed his need for gainful employment to support his family, he received three job offers that same night. He began working in his trade again as a master electrician.

We continued to seek God by attending worship services, substance abuse support meetings and Bible study. My husband told me that the genuine love of the people and the Word of God are what delivered him from alcohol and drugs. He never went to a rehab of any kind and is still delivered today. He was later hired by a major telecommunications company and was assigned to work in the same building where I worked before I retired. The Word of God says, "Seek ye first the kingdom of God and His righteousness, and all these things shall be added unto you." God had given my husband the desire of his heart, gainful employment.

We went to work together and came back home together every day. My husband reminded me that we needed to spend more time in the Word of God so that we could stay delivered and continue to grow spiritually. I agreed and we decided that we would use our 30-minute lunch break to have Bible study. Every day we would find a quiet spot to have Bible study. My husband asked me to teach him the Word of God since I was the minister. Sometimes he would even refer to me as his pastor. It was very humbling to me that my husband respected the anointing of God on my life. He later shared with me that another vital part of his deliverance was the realization that I truly loved him because I didn't give up on him after all that he had taken me through.

We continued to study the Word of God, even though we were no longer able to attend the substance abuse support meetings because of my husband's new job hours. I became his support by feeding him the Word of God on a daily basis. We still had challenges in our marriage, but the alcohol and drugs were history. My husband had become a new creation and we had to get to know each other all over again.

The first three years of our marriage had been a living hell for me. Because of his addiction, I had become the head of the household. Therefore, I had to learn how to submit to this new man who had become the new head of our household. By attending the men's ministry meetings with Pastor Dollar, my husband learned his duties as the king and priest of his home and proceeded to share them with me. Since he is saved, sanctified and filled with the Holy Ghost, he could and can hear from God too. As a matter of fact, as the head of the household, it is his job to get instructions from the Father on how to run his household and take care of his family. He advised me that God gives him specific instructions, and that he doesn't have to try to figure things out for himself.

It was a challenge for me to begin to trust my husband again after having to do everything myself to keep a roof over our heads. I could only see what was wrong with my husband until one day he responded to me by saying, "Honey, you have to see me whole." I continued to stay prayerful, and God reassured me that my husband was no longer bound but free to hear His voice. The Holy Spirit convicted me for trying to be in control, and assured me that my husband had not only been delivered but had been restored to his rightful place as the king and priest of our home.

I began to be slow to speak and quick to hear what the Spirit of God was saying to me. I asked the Holy Spirit to speak through me and to teach me how to love my husband. I thought I had forgiven him, but the Holy Spirit revealed to me that deep down inside I felt that my husband still owed me something for all that I had been through. There was a residue of unforgiveness that lay dormant in my spirit and I needed to clean house. I realized that I was still going through the deliverance process myself. We were still living in the condo when his mother came from Miami, Florida to visit. She brought with her a beautiful pants suit along with a beautiful card that read, "Thank you for not giving up on my son." It melted my heart and encouraged me in the faith to see how proud she was of her son and how grateful she was to God for his deliverance, and most of all, that she realized how much I loved him. She is a powerful woman of God who had been praying for her son a long time.

Cynthia R. Rolle, a native of Miami, Florida, has served as an ordained itinerant elder of the African Methodist Episcopal Church since 1998. She is presently serving as senior pastor at St. Paul A.M.E. Church in Dublin, Georgia. She graduated with honors in 2003 from Turner Theological Seminary and the Interdenominational Theological Center where she received a Master of Divinity Degree with a concentration in Christian Education. Her testimony is found in Galatians 2:20, "I am crucified with Christ: nevertheless I live, yet not I, but Christ lives in me; and the life which I now live in the flesh I live by the faith of the Son of God, who loved me, and gave himself for me."

My Journey
Mary Helen Nickelberry

"Unto thee, O LORD, do I lift up my soul." ~ Psalm 25:1

Life is a journey - begun each day with a prayer of thankfulness for the night and a look toward the day with hope for living a life for oneself but also with the desire to share what I have with others as the need presents itself - a journey inward and a journey outward.

I could reminisce and review my 89 years' journey to the present, but I prefer to begin talking about now, the present and breath in the sweet essence of the journey through which God's grace brought me to today. It is a journey that has been flanked by prayer, hope and joy for the "Grace that is sufficient" for all things.

Journeying inward to that place where I reach down deep into my very being --- my soul --- is the way my daily journey begins. It is the place where I meet Jesus in prayer and Bible study; where I often find new meaning to previously read scriptures and where my very soul cries out in joy with these revelations. The very core feeling lets me know that my journey is as real as breathing in and breathing out. It is feeling and knowing the unconditional love of the savior. However, it does not stop there. It leads me to the desire to share that love with others either in a thoughtful way or sometimes in a prayer whispered for a sick friend or neighbor or one who might be in a job search or for a specific request from a member of my Circle

31

of Care. My journey outward reflects service beyond self.

The prayers, worship and fellowship of my Christian sisters and brothers undergird my journey as we meet regularly for worship and as we reach out together in ministry and mission to our community and the world. We find joy in the commitments we make to know and listen for God's leading in the daily challenges in our journey together. It is from here that we celebrate and engage the journey outward to our families, community and to the world.

Today, no matter how challenging my journey, with God's help, I reach out to new opportunities that lie before me. Now is the time to discover new songs of hope, joy and peace and bring them to the world that is in such desperate need of that music.

Mary Helen Nickleberry is a native of New Orleans, Louisiana and a graduate of Dillard University and Fordham University. She completed additional educational studies in Geriatrics at U. C. Berkerly and is an active church leader, facilitator and Bible teacher.

By and By
Marion Smith

"Lo, children are a heritage of the LORD: and the fruit of the womb is his reward." ~ Psalm 127:3

Many years ago in a little southern country church the choir often sang a song resounding how we would better understand the lessons of life "by and by." It is my honor to share with you today a "by and by" testimony from my first-born son.

It was just an ordinary day, no special celebration, when my son dropped a card in my mailbox along with a collection of Jet magazines. As I read the card, I reflected:

My son could not have written this note as a teenager because that was the period when I was known as the "meanest woman" on the planet and a wicked strict mother who had "no fun" rules and long lists of chores to be done and forbidden behaviors like, "no hanging out on corners." He had no idea that my attitudes and behaviors were deeply rooted in fear and a mother's desperate attempt to guard and protect a black child born in the aftermath of the horrific killing of a young teenage black male, Emmitt Till. It is quite understandable that through the eyes of my son, my excessive guarded behavior would not win a popularity contest.

So at age 77, I stood reading a special note of testimony from my 51-year-older son. I've gotten other validations from all of my

33

children in previous years and my heart is deeply touched by their words.

My older son wrote:
Mom,

I wanted to take time to tell you what a shining example you are. You continue to raise the bar for yourself and we follow. I don't know anyone like Ms. "M." You are amazing. You are the epitome of African American pride!!! Here, here!!! Looking back over my life, you are the best mom that anyone could ever have."

Love,
Oding

So, I end my testimony by offering a word of encouragement to young parents today. With maturation comes knowledge, understanding and wisdom as related to life's challenges. As a parent, we can mature in faith and trust in God to direct us in releasing fear and begin parenting from a position of courage and strength. Also, with maturation the child comes to understand the challenges and responsibilities that accompany parenthood. So keep the faith -- - stick with it. Stay on the job and know that the time will come when your child will reach the state of maturity to acknowledge your works. Be assured ---- it will come by and by.

Marion Smith, a native of Oakland, California is a graduate of San Francisco State University with a Master's of Education from Cal State Hayward. She was a school principal and retired educator from the Oakland Public School System. Ms. Smith is a licensed spiritual counseling coach, master teacher of African Stories and a charter member of Toastmasters.

Standing On The Promises of God
Summer Joel

"For now we really live, since you are standing firm in the Lord."
~ 1 Thessalonians 3:8

Song: *"Standing – standing - standing on the promises of Christ my Savior. Standing – standing -- standing on the promises of God."*

In a recent church service, my pastor asked the question, "Where is God at work in your life?" Just then without saying a word, a man stood up within the congregation who had recently suffered a heart attack. I could see that he was still recovering, but he couldn't help but stand as a testimony to God's healing power in his life. It was evident to all in the congregation that he was still standing-standing on the promises of God!

It was then that I reflected on my own testimony. I had been sexually abused at about the age of eight-years-old. I say about because I have blocked out and have little recollection of my young life at that time. I can recall few things until after the age of 12, so I've had to pinpoint when the sexual abuse actually happened. What I do remember is who violated me (my babysitter), the person the enemy used to steal so much out of my young soul. And although it's difficult to recall, I still remember some of the acts and even the odor of the sins that I was coerced to do at that time. The four years from ages 8-12 seem to run together as one big blur until the day when my parents began noticing that some things (food and alcohol mostly) were missing from our house. They finally realized that it was my babysitter. She had been violating us all! Although I didn't realize until years later, God's sovereign hand had reached down and said, "That's enough," and before I knew it, she was gone out of my life - as my babysitter.

The next significant event that I can remember is at the age 13. I had gone from playing with dolls to playing with boys. I didn't understand it then, but what would you expect to happen for a girl who had been having sex since the age of eight and with a female? So much was stolen from me with each act of rape. Years later I felt as if my very soul had been stolen. I've heard it said that most of a person's development begins at the crucial ages from 8-12, and those years, experiences, memories, had been stolen right out from under me.

Truth be told, much of my life I feel as though I've been floundering, like I'm constantly struggling/fighting to stay above water, trying to regain my footing (that which I lost). The last six years, however, have been a time of God's providential healing power in my life (another book). As a matter of fact, in early 2001, it had been prophesied to me that I would receive the best miracle of my life, outside of my salvation. My miracle was that I received my healing and it began manifesting that same year and is still continuing. Like the man in the beginning of my story who stood up, I am still in recovery.

In March of 2005, I opened my Bible to the book of Joel. I sensed strongly that I was reading more than just a story in the Bible. My spirit was hearing a promise from God. It was His promise to me that He would restore everything that had been stolen. As I read further in Joel 2:24-27, He told me that He would restore that which was taken away - eaten up by the "swarming locusts, the consuming locusts and the chewing locust," as the Word says. Locusts are insects that eat up everything that's alive; they are creatures of destruction. But it's only when everything is dead and has been destroyed, God

ONLY can renew life! I began to relate the words that God spoke to me to what I felt had been taken from my life.

All I can say is that God's promises to me are my only real source of comfort and hope - hope of the great and powerful things that He will use from what happened to me for His glory. I stand on His word as He tells me "Summer, I will work all things together for your good since you love me, and are called according to my purpose" (Romans 8:28, paraphrased).

I'm still healing. But it's in this experience, that I learning and experiencing God's true healing power. Since one of my first experiences with love and trust in relationships was broken, God's re-teaching me. He's teaching me about the importance of relationships (healthy and divine relationships). Most importantly, what it is to have a relationship with Him, what that means and how I couldn't possibly heal or even live without Him. He's teaching me about real love, His Love for me and how He wants me to love Him. He's teaching me how to love myself and properly how to love others - not the sexual way in which I learned. God's re-teaching me about trust, trust in Him to fulfill, to supply, provide and direct everything that I would possibly need. He's teaching me how to trust MYSELF and to trust others. In all these areas God is working out my restoration and I'm taking back what the enemy has stolen!

Although, I'm still going through the re-learning process, God has given me His divine grace, mercy and spiritual vision to see that He will use my experience to bless and free others for His glory. Even though I admit that it hasn't all been easy, God gives me the courage to lean on His promises again. He helps me to understand that He'll never leave me nor forsake me. Through it all, I am still standing and some days I can even dance!!!!!

"Standing- standing-standing on the promises of Christ my Savior, Standing-standing on the promises of God!"

Summer Joel is currently residing in the Atlanta, Georgia area. She earned her Bachelor's degree from Saint Leo University. She is pursuing her seminary training at Luther Rice University where her major is Biblical Counseling. She serves in various ministries as well as a minister in training at Greenforest Community Baptist Church in Decatur, Georgia.

The Horizon
Vera Ousley

"Wait on the LORD; be of good courage, and He shall strengthen your heart; Wait, I say, on the LORD!" ~ Psalm 27:14

The beginning of 2004 was an empty room with unpainted walls and bare floors; fresh, clean and free of unpleasant odors. To ease life's journey, the space was cleared of old luggage with broken clasps and no wheels. The cobwebs, dusty hurts and angst were wiped away or packed and placed in a beautiful chest, not to be forgotten, but not in the way. Broken things were repaired or replaced. Shutters, that kept the room dark, were removed and the windows were cleaned to let in light and the wonders of nature. The windows were new and they opened to the outside so the gifts, talents and love within could be shared. The chimney was swept and the fireplace was in good working order, waiting for a fire to be lit. It was a room ready to be filled with everything! Neutrals for a solid base; fabrics and textiles for warmth and comfort; rich colors to soothe and heal; bright spots for happiness, excitement and imagination; some treasured things that bring joy and spark memories. Touches of black would have to be placed here and there to ground the room and give it depth. I was being molded, shaped and honed to be able to make this room beautiful and Spirit filled. I wanted to jump in - start anywhere and work until my eyes and heart told me it was done, but God's order must prevail. I had to follow His lead, pray over choices, move at His pace and thank Him all along the way.

June of 2005 came and the room was still empty, a little dusty and waiting. Horizons can be deceptive and farther away than the natural eye perceives it to be. We must wait on God's time. Spirits that are afraid of the light have tried, are still trying to keep this room empty. Unwanted guests staged an invasion; the plumbing is succumbing to the weight of age; things tried don't work out, some of the wires to the power source have been severed. I was standing there waiting to use the gifts given, to share the light within. Standing and waiting.

December 2006 and the room is starting to take shape. The spirits have been banished that raised a ruckus and fought to deny the desire for beauty, comfort and a sanctuary for fellowship. They could not prevail against a child who has surrendered to the Most High God. They could not prevail against a child who has forged a solid bond of trust that relies on the Lamb for guidance and wisdom. The room is not complete, there are still things missing and repairs are in progress. But the light is shining in and I have learned that the gifts can still be shared and life can be celebrated even though the project is in process. 2007 is dawning.

December 2007 and the room has fulfilled much of its potential. An observer can easily see the beauty and the light within. Plants, friends and animals are nurtured and thrive in this room. The room extends an open invitation to come in, get comfortable and together share the gifts that the Father has given us. Let's bask in the brilliance of some of the colors and the calm of others. Let's admire the treasures and share the stories behind them. A few dreams have been fulfilled in this room and other dreams and hopes are just over the horizon. The room compels that gratitude for blessings are expressed with joy and expectancy. The Spirit dwells here. The room is surrendered to the Spirit and the hope of realizing other dreams is not punctuated by a question mark. It took a while to get here and some of the roads to this room were hard to travel. The room is a reflection of the changes that the Spirit of the Lamb within has made. I give glory unto God for the journey.

Vera Ousley was born in a small town in Mississippi and reared in a suburb of Memphis, Tennessee. She attended Jackson State University and moved to California after graduation. She lived in California for 18 years before relocating to Atlanta, Georgia. She is a financial analyst by profession. Her faith and love has been tested but endures.

Precious Memories
Lisa Harrison

"I have been reminded of your sincere faith, which first lived in your grandmother Lois and in your mother Eunice and, I am persuaded, now lives in you also." ~ 2 Timothy 1:5

I was born in Bakersfield, California - let's just say, "a few" years ago. Bakersfield summers are extremely hot. Imagine triple digit desert dry days where one can actually see heat waves if you look far enough down the road. I understood God's importance in our lives because my earliest memories include walking to church along dirt sidewalks on hot summer days. Even then, I was glad to know that I belonged to God and I don't recall a time in my life when I didn't feel the comfort of His presence.

As a child, I spent a lot of time with my maternal grandmother. She had tremendous influence on me. She lost her battle with ovarian cancer in October of 1981 and I still think about her almost on a daily basis. Whenever I hear about a new development that increases the chances of surviving ovarian cancer, I still wonder if such treatment might have helped her. Grandma was an exceptionally wise, strong and principled woman and her faith walk was evident. Without a doubt, her influence on me began before I have conscious memory of it. She wasn't one to give frivolous verbal compliments, but she didn't hesitate to acknowledge one's talent and her belief that it should be used to serve God and to be prudent in one's living. She clearly communicated to me that she thought I was smart, an especially good reader, and she expected me to use it productively. Now I knew Grandma's opinion about people who were "smart in their books but didn't have a lick of common sense" and those who were lazy, so she didn't have any trouble getting me on board with her program.

I was assigned lengthy speeches for church programs and I was expected to recite them perfectly. She didn't tolerate careless errors on the Bible memory verse we learned each week in Sunday school. During her Women's Mission meetings, I was often assigned to read aloud to the group. I also read the letters she received from her many siblings who lived all over the country and I had to write her responses. I would also read the Bible to her while she quilted. Grandma admired my talent, and yet, I wonder if she knew that I felt the same way about her talents. She only had a third grade education but she had such wisdom and she was fearless. She often shared the story of how she chopped cotton to support the family when my grandfather died and left her to raise eight children shortly after they had moved to California during the Depression. My mother, the youngest, wasn't quite two years old at that time. Even though she had not wanted to leave her family in Oklahoma and move to California all those years ago, I never heard regret or self-pity in her voice. She had a gift for embracing people and was the epitome of a Christian matriarch. I always aspired to be like that.

My mother was a single parent for much of my childhood. She worked as a nurse at the local county hospital and when she would leave dressed in her white nurse uniform, including the stiffly starched hat, I remember being so proud of her. Grandma told us repeatedly how hard Mom worked to put herself through nursing school so she could support our family. Even then, I understood the sacrifices Mom was making. I remember thinking that one day, my sister and I would be old enough to help Mom and she wouldn't have to work so hard. Mom has been quiet, but steadfast in her support for me, especially after I, too, became a single parent. She has helped me in ways she wasn't required, and I truly appreciate it.

Mom was blessed to have sisters who helped rear us during those early years. Aunt Grace's house was like a second home. We loved to go there because Aunt Grace indulged us and she was always baking wonderful things to eat. We spent summers in Oakland with Aunt Sarah and she also loved to spoil us. When I graduated from college and moved to Oakland, I lived with Aunt Sarah until I married.

With that backdrop, our immediate and extended family made it abundantly clear that education is important. I was a good student and enjoyed school, so going to college wasn't a tough sell for me. I am currently pursuing a doctorate degree and truly enjoying the experience. Even as a young undergraduate student, I thought about someday earning a doctorate. I didn't make firm plans to do so, but I've always seen it as an attainable goal. However, after earning my bachelor's degree, getting married, starting a family and a career, my educational goals were adjusted accordingly. I focused on completing the classes necessary to complete my teaching license.

While my family initially shaped me and encouraged my pursuit of education, along the way I've been blessed to encounter many wonderful educators and role models. I would love to have an opportunity to let these teachers know how they touched my life. For example, my 3rd grade teacher, Miss Acorn, was an avid traveler. She had visited many exotic and adventurous places. In her effort to spark her students' interest and curiosity about the world, she would share pictures, costumes and artifacts from her travels. It would literally bring those places alive for us. I loved to read books about the places Miss Acorn traveled. My 6th grade teacher, Mr. Smith, was awesome. He was my first male teacher, and we all thought this guy was so cute, hip and cool. He made learning relevant and fun. I recall a social studies lesson where we built a paper mache town on several large tables in the center of the classroom. Each student received a plot of land and an occupation. We learned the responsibilities we had as contributing citizens of the town. We also learned the realities of land location, investing, the weather, politics and the economy.

By the time I reached high school, I was beginning to think about becoming a teacher. I especially liked my business education teacher, Mrs. Kelner, and she confirmed my career choice. She was the height of professionalism. She was always friendly and enthusiastic, but firm and relentless in her expectation that we achieve excellence! I took several classes from her including typing (on brand new IBM Selectric II typewriters!), accounting and stenography. Now, didn't that take you down memory lane? Enrollment in the stenography class was considered to be a privilege because Mrs. Kelner only recommended her top students. Since I did well in Mrs. Kelner's classes, she recommended me for my first job at Bank of America when I was in the 11th grade. I was thrilled and so was my family! I worked my way through college at Bank of America using the office skills that Mrs. Kelner taught me in high school. I've typed this paper and countless others using the techniques she taught me. What a gift it is to touch someone's life in such a positive way!

After I completed my bachelor's degree, I moved to Oakland, California and shortly thereafter began attending Allen Temple Baptist Church. I know God led me to Allen Temple because I immediately felt at home and I didn't know a soul there when I began attending. This was a huge step for me because prior to that, I had only attended two churches in my life; my family's home church in Bakersfield and during college in San Jose, I attended the church where my cousins were already members. I can't begin to describe the spiritual and personal growth I experienced during those years. Pastor J. Alfred Smith is truly a dynamic man of God. I could immediately relate to his sermons because he focused on teaching and helping people to understand their commitment as a Christian. I also met many other mentors and role models who embraced me over the years. People like Dr. Regina Anderson, Mrs. Albertha Lastie, Mrs. Marie Johnson, Mother Young and too many others to name here truly define Christian service. Pastor Smith always referred to the congregation as the Allen Temple Family. Because

I'm from a large, close-knit extended family, I recognized sincere familial connection and I definitely felt it there!

Recently, I attended the retirement reception for a counselor with whom I had worked shortly after moving to Georgia. This counselor had been at the same elementary school long enough to have seen the children of her previous students attend the school. Although I always knew she was a special person, I was moved to tears as person after person spoke of how she had touched their lives. Despite a caseload that exceeded levels where one could expect to be able to really be effective, she had been able to make a lot of people know that she cared about them and their ability to be the best they could be. I remember thinking that would be a priceless legacy to leave. Not only did she do her best, she helped others reach their potential. I was so touched by this because in my experience the leaders that I have most admired truly cared about people. I aspire to follow in their footsteps.

The Lord has truly blessed my life and I want to be careful to always give Him the glory! I've had the help and favor of so many wonderful people during my life's journey! Although I've always appreciated them, I've grown to treasure them even more; especially as the years pass and many have left the land of the living.

Lisa Harrison was born and raised in California. She accepted Jesus Christ as her personal savior when she was a young child. Lisa has been an educator for more than 25 years. She is an avid reader and also enjoys writing. She and her family currently reside in metro Atlanta. She is the mother of two sons.

Transition to Purpose

Singing As I Go
Robin Dial

"For I know the plans I have for you," declares the LORD, "plans to prosper you and not to harm you, plans to give you hope and a future." ~ Jeremiah 29:11

In my 42 years of life I can truly say that God has always had His hand on me. From an early age I was brought up knowing and celebrating Jesus. As I ventured out into adulthood and married my friend at the tender age of 20, little did I know that the journey began in the innocence of our dating. "King Jesus was a-listening" even then to the desires of my heart as I prayed for what I wanted and believed could be a perfect family - a loving husband, a couple of kids, a home and career. Little did I know that "Every time I felt the Spirit" it was the precious hand of Jesus softly telling me to put on my "Traveling Shoes."

You see, God had a bigger plan, not the simple little life that I imagined in my head. Even though God had given me the loving husband, two healthy and handsome sons, a home and a teaching career in a Christian school which would touch countless children and their families, what I did not know was that His plan was to entrust ministry to me and my family. He wanted to use us to win

47

souls for Christ; He wanted to use us in the lives of young people and young families. God called my husband into the ministry and how many of you sisters know that meant He called me as well. My prayer and my song became "Stand by Me" and "I want Jesus to Walk With Me."

What a mighty God we serve! What I love about God is when you realize you are on the journey often times you are almost at the finish line. I believe that no matter how large or small someone may consider your journey, it is just that, your journey. God's journey for your life is but a small piece of the puzzle for His ultimate plan. However, what we fail to realize is that without our small piece the puzzle forever remains unfinished.

As I sit back and marvel at God for choosing me to be the helpmate to a man of God; as I sit back and think of helping to build God's kingdom in a mighty way, all I can say is, "My good Lord done been here." I thank Him each day for being here, for being in my life, for using me. The journey ain't over; it's only just begun.

_____

Robin Dial is currently pursuing a degree in Counseling and Human Services at Atlanta Christian College. She has taught Pre-K and Kindergarten at Greenforest McCalep Christian Academy for over 15 years. She is married to her college sweetheart, Rev. Steven Dial. They are blessed with two handsome sons, Steven and Micah.

A Change Has Come Over Me
Edna Hartwell

"He will bring you new life and support you in your old age." ~
Ruth 4:15.

      In spite of all the years we have lived and the experiences we recall, there are special turning points in our lives that become clear defining moments that shape us into who we are. Such moments have boldly exploded in my spirit that set me on a clear path to achieving a specific mission. Some might say it was the Spirit of the Lord or the voice of God. The experience always renders me weak and completely shaken.

      As my daughter and I walked down the street of this beautiful neighborhood, I was mesmerized by the magnificent homes and the details of the landscaping and tree-lined driveways. We walked a little further and I saw my house; but at the moment I could not recall why this was my home. I couldn't recall having made the purchase and I didn't know anything about the inside.

      The house was set on a hill and had columns across the front with about seven steps leading to the front door. The yard was well manicured like all the others, but I couldn't recall how it had occurred. In spite of my apprehension, Feleshia and I walked across the grass to the front steps. As we ascended to the front door, she asked me to help her with her sweater because she felt a chill.

The front door opened to a beautiful two-story foyer with a banister overlooking the front entrance and a sunken living room off to the left. We were immediately swept up in the ambience and excitement of such an incredible place and did not close the door. After entering further into the foyer we were confronted by a wolf at the top of the stairs. His eyes were fire-like and he caught my gaze as he pounced to the marble floor right in front of us. In spite of our overwhelming fear, we didn't move. The animal fled through the front door and down the street.

Fear immediately dissipated and we stepped further into the house only to be confronted by a second wolf at the top of the stairs. As fear started to rise in me again, somehow I sensed that if I could look at the beast my faith would overcome my fear and he would no longer be a threat. As he jumped from the top of the stairs, he fell dead at my feet. A third wolf was prepared to attack from the Living Room. Feleshia stood behind me, and I could feel the spirit of God rise up in me and through me in the form of a green fluorescent light that permeated the space between me and the beast. Though the beast was not human, he spoke in a human voice as the light engulfed him. "A child of God. A man from Nazareth." As he fell dead at my feet, the fourth and final beast ran from the house and the door closed.

Having been raised in an environment where it was common for my grandfather, father, uncles and male cousins to have multiple relationships during marriage, I was easy prey to wolves. I found them, sheltered them, fed them, and allowed them to take advantage of every good thing that God blessed me with. This dream or spiritual awakening was clearly a major defining moment in my life and as I started the process of assessing the wolves that had clearly violated who I am, I was able to assign a face to each beast that fled my imaginary home.

At age 28, I was well into my career with IBM and truly enjoying life. Unfortunately, this was the age that my family started questioning when I would settle down and start a family. After looking at my options from a worldly standpoint, I chose someone with a similar career from a decent family and whom I thought would be a decent father. How I wish the dream had occurred prior to the marriage. The seven years was filled with infidelity, heartbreak and no romance. In spite of the pain and challenges in the marriage, I wanted to be a strong woman and stay with my husband. My mother and grandmother were able to hang in there. "Father, I know I can do this."

At 31-years-old I thought I was well proportioned; weighing 135 pounds and 5'4." Within six weeks after the birth of my child I was back to my normal size and in my bikini. I was exercising and staying in shape; taking care of the baby, and everything else around the house, but my husband did not find me attractive. I tried romantic dinners and special weekends away but nothing worked. His response was always, "I don't find you attractive. You are too fat."

I continued to persevere. My husband wanted his own automobile dealership. In my mind I thought this would be my opportunity to demonstrate my commitment to him and the marriage. I worked while he attended a special training program with Ford Motor Company. After two years, he had made it and was placed in a Ford Dealership in Georgia. This was going to be an opportunity for us to work together and really build the family. In preparation for the grand opening celebration, his family drove in from Texas.

What an exciting moment. I was so proud as I listened to the mayor introducing my husband and his team. As my husband stepped to the podium, I stood with my head held high, my shoulders were perfectly squared, and all of my teeth were showing through the wide grin on my face. "That is MY husband. I helped him to raise the enormous amount of money to finance this place. Look at what we have done." With this last vain moment of personal praise, I realized that the ceremony was almost over. He had introduced the administrative staff, the sales reps, management team, paint and body shop; and even the janitors....but not his wife. "Is this really happening?" Yep. The ceremony is over. The punch and cookies are all gone and the crowd has disbursed. I could not have been more embarrassed if I had been standing on the side of the road nude wearing cowboy boots.

As we drove in separate vehicles to our condo away from home, I had to suck it up, swallow my pride and pretend that everything was alright. "His family is here," I said to myself. "We've got to entertain them. I can do this." The brother took a detour and did not come in until the next morning. He chose *this* weekend to tell me he wanted a divorce.

All of the funds for investing in the business were now in his possession. In my trusting innocence, our stocks, bonds, and other financial accounts were written with the word "OR" instead of "AND." He liquidated everything that we owned and left me with nothing. Through my tears and despair I called a close girlfriend who had attended the grand opening the day before. She just happened to work for the State's Attorney General. She listened quietly and said, "It's 3:00. You can cry until 5:00 and then you call me back."

On Monday morning she had crafted a plan to freeze all assets of the dealership until my investments were returned. The plan was presented to Ford Motor Company and within two weeks, I had my money and the ex was ousted from the dealership. *The door was left open for the wolf to leave.* He left on his own accord and I did not have to face the stigma of giving up on my marriage. The love had left long before he walked away, but for years I chose to walk the path of "being a set" because this is what we are taught. We are expected to grow up, get married and have kids. Nobody bothers to teach us how to choose a husband or to be a wife. We simply mirror what we see in our churches, communities and our own families. "Deacon Jones fathered Aunt Lucy's daughter and everybody is aware of it but everyone pretends that Uncle Amos is really her daddy." "What about Pastor Brown who has children in the little country churches where he is the every-other-Sunday preacher?" To avoid the "mess" in the church, Big Mama simply stopped going.

We know the scriptures. We teach the scriptures but from generation to generation we are still "playing church" and breeding wolves that can only be chased away by truly and authentically living the Word of God. It is not okay for us (black folks) to continue to lift up our preachers who have violated the sanctity of their vows to God, their wives and the church.

Feeling alone and no longer included in our old circles, I longed for marriage. By now I was deeply involved in the church. I was a Sunday school teacher and assistant director of Children's Chapel; so it seemed natural that I would have a special attraction to someone in the church. After three years of being single, I moved back to Texas, met and married one whom the family thought was the perfect man for me: a minister. On our wedding day we fought over who was going to be my beneficiary. He left the reception before we cut the cake because "the cable man" was coming to connect his TV.

There was never a day of peace in the marriage. My daughter was not allowed to speak in the presence of adults and took her meals alone at the breakfast table or alone in her room. We drove an hour and a half to his country church in complete silence.

Two years and three separations later, I had survived physical, mental, sexual abuse and I allowed him to squander every dime I owned. The last time he tied my nightgown around my throat, I simply said, "You may as well kill me. Death has to be better than this."

I started to quietly and strategically steal away enough money to leave. On a warm Saturday morning I packed my daughter's Barbie dolls, toys, clothes and as many of my things as would fit in my car and headed back to Atlanta. For six months I slept on a friend's sofa and my daughter stayed with her dad (who had since remarried). I found a job as a part-time receptionist for $6.00 an hour. I traveled almost an hour one way to work and sat in traffic another hour to return.

I longed to see my daughter but couldn't visit her at her dad's. Talking on the phone was not enough so we decided that we would identify a place in the mall that we called "Home." Home for us was a white plastic table in the food court in South DeKalb Mall. If someone was sitting at our "Home" when we arrived, we would wait for them to leave. This was such joy for us. We had each other and we had peace.

Within six months I was blessed with a better job and Feleshia and I moved into a one bedroom apartment just before Thanksgiving. We were invited to the home of the dear friend that had seen me through the challenges with the first husband and the dealership. They had moved into an incredible million dollar mansion in an exclusive neighborhood that featured tennis courts, an indoor pool and every possible amenity.

That night as we drove back to our tiny apartment, I was thinking about the wonderful time that we had experienced with Greg and Juanita; and at the same time I was concerned that Feleshia would be a little sad that our lifestyle was not comparable. As I continued to drive, she put her hand in mine and said, "One day we will have a house like that." She was right. The wolves are all clearly identified and gone from my life. Their individual exits from my life will continue as a continuation of this journey.

It is no secret what God can do. What He's done for others.....He'll do for you.

Edna Hartwell was born in Hillsboro, Texas. She is a graduate of Paul Quinn College and is currently the president and founder of ConTech Design Group, Inc; a construction engineering design firm that specializes in school safety, security and technology. She is the mother of Feleshia Sams, who is also co-owner of the firm. They have offices in Atlanta, Washington, D.C., Houston and Savannah.

A Little Talk With Jesus
Dr. Judy W. Hollis

"But Jesus said, Suffer little children, and forbid them not, to come unto me: for of such is the kingdom of heaven." ~ Matthew 19:14

My journey began at Manley Taylor Elementary School where I attended third grade. During my third grade year, I could be described as a very shy and insecure little girl. My teacher who appeared to be very harsh and insensitive to not only my needs but also other students as well, taught with a forceful hand. My parents taught me to respect my teacher and learn.

My father never attended public school and my mother finished the eighth grade. My father taught himself to read by reading the Bible and requiring my six brothers and sisters to read the Bible to him. Reading became intimidating and helped to create insecurities about reading and especially reading out loud.

One day my teacher called me up to the black board to sound out the helping verbs. As I began to walk to the board fear gripped me and I did not speak a word. My teacher, who had no tolerance, screamed at me and with a ruler beat me in front of the whole class. This was one of the most hurtful experiences in my life. As I sat back in my seat, I cried uncontrollably and remembered whenever

I saw my mother crying she would pray to God. As I cried in my desk, I began to have a little talk with Jesus:

> "Dear God, I want to be a teacher, and if you help me become a teacher I will love all my students, I'll be kind to them and I will teach them to read. I will not be mean and I won't embarrass them and I will help them to learn to read. Please help me in school this year. Please teach me to read. I know you can because my mother said you can do anything but fail..."

God answers prayers. Even my very innocent third grade prayer was answered.

I finished school with a high school diploma, Bachelor's of Science in Elementary Education, Master's of Arts in Elementary Education, Educational Specialist degree in Leadership, Doctorate in Theology and finally a Reading Specialist degree. I am certified to teach reading to elementary, middle and high school students. I have been awarded for my success in teaching reading to the lower 25% of students, with a 95% pass rate. God has given me a vision to write books that will help parents and teachers teach children how to read. A little talk with Jesus made it possible for me to walk into my destiny and bless others with my own insecurities and fears. The Lord uses what we think is a weakness to strengthen us for His glory. Today my motto remains, "I can do all things through Christ who strengthens me."

Dr. Judy W. Hollis is a reading specialist for Orange County Public Schools in Orlando, Florida. She is the CEO of Hope Enterprise, Inc. where she is an evangelist, self-publisher, consultant, motivational speaker and literacy coach for parents. She is a mother and wife and enjoys reading in her spare time.

All God's Children Need Traveling Shoes
Mae Alice Reggy-Mamo, Ph.D.

"How beautiful on the mountains are the feet of those who bring good news, who proclaim peace, who bring good tidings, who proclaim salvation, who say to Zion, Your God reigns!" Isaiah 52:7

My head throbbed with excitement as I rolled the cart piled high with luggage through the exit door at Jomo Kenyatta International Airport in 1976. Overwhelmed with emotion, I walked with my husband and three small daughters through the heavy, steel door into the ululating crowd. Within minutes, a host of relatives and friends gathered around welcoming us with brisk handshakes. My husband's older brother stepped forward and wrapped his arms around him and in their home language (*Dholuo*) said: *"Wuod mama, isechopo* ...Son of my mother, you have returned!" The two brothers embraced.

My first taste of Kenya came when we visited in August 1969. But this time was different; we had sold our house and shipped everything to Kenya. For my husband, Dr. John Odhiambo Reggy (now deceased); this was a long-awaited homecoming. Having earned a Ph.D. in Political Science, he was now coming back home to settle after 20 years in the USA. For me, this was an answer to prayer. As a child, I had dreamed of going to Africa and finding my ancestral roots. I remembered a vivacious woman from our church — affectionately called Mother Stafford — who had traveled to Nigeria as a missionary when I was around five years old. She came back and told vivid stories of remote African villages where women pounded yams simultaneously and children frolicked under swaying banana trees. She'd said, "We weren't born in Africa, but we're cut from the same cloth." Her words stuck in my mind. From age five on, I remember praying I would some day live in Africa where Mother Stafford said black men were government leaders and determined the destiny of their people.

That first afternoon, relatives flooded the family home to celebrate our return. They came one by one, greeting us as they entered the house. Soon the living room was packed and benches were put out in the yard where relatives sat in clusters quenching their thirst with bottles of warm soda. Almost immediately the women connected with me. Many of them reminded me of my kinfolk back in Montclair, New Jersey where I grew up. I remember that first night. Although jet-lagged, I laid my head down on the pillow and whispered a prayer, "Thank you, Lord. I'm in Africa at last – the land of my ancestors!" Little did I know the plans God had for me.

Growing up, I attended Trinity Temple Church of God in Christ, then a small storefront church where my dad served as assistant pastor for more than 40 years. At that time, I'd often hear church folks speak disparagingly about education. *"The letter killeth,"* they'd say. But during my teen years, a progressive young preacher who had just graduated from New York University was appointed pastor. He inspired me to achieve academic excellence and make a difference. After graduating from high school, I earned a B.A. in English from Douglass College, Rutgers University (1963). During my college years, I traveled to Puerto Rico for an intercultural exchange program. Once my traveling shoes were on, there was no taking them off. Commissioned by President John F. Kennedy, I served as a Peace Corps Volunteer in Turkey from 1963-1965 and during the summer of 1964 I traveled via ship to visit a Christian family in Egypt. On returning to the USA, I earned an

M.A. in Education from Howard University (1970) and a Ph.D. in Education from University of Maryland (1976). By the time I left for Kenya in 1976, I was a wife, mother of three, educator, lay-minister and world traveler.

Downtown Nairobi abounds with grand office buildings, supermarkets, high-rise apartments, cyber cafes, retail clothing stores, gas stations, barbershops, hair salons, churches, mosques, restaurants and hotels. My first job in Nairobi was teaching English at the United States International University located in the Mayfield Hotel complex. I enjoyed working with such diligent students, but the Lord was making it clear to me that he was calling me into full-time ministry. A year later Evangel Publishing House was looking for a senior editor. I took the job and enjoyed editing in-coming manuscripts, working with emerging African writers and writing a few short books myself, but the Lord was urging me to fulfill His calling on my life. One afternoon, a Kenyan couple approached me. They had received a prayer request that the United Bible Societies (UBS) was looking for someone to write biblical text in simple English for new literates. By that time, Evangel had moved their downtown office and having just given birth to a fourth baby daughter, I found the morning commute difficult. So I applied for the job with UBS and they hired me. At the time I really did not know what I was getting into, but the Lord did and He made it clear that He was sending me to the nations. Years earlier, my pastor had prophetically uttered these words: "Mae, the Lord pulled back a curtain and allowed me to see a whole panorama of people and places around you. The Lord is sending you to many nations." These words had now come to pass.

For the next 24 years (from 1979-2004) I worked with (UBS) as Literacy Consultant for Africa. While working with UBS, I conducted training workshops in more than 24 African countries, including Ghana, Togo, Nigeria, Liberia, Benin, Burkina Faso, Cameroon, and Côte d'Ivoire, Congo-Brazzaville, Democratic Republic of Congo, Rwanda, Burundi, Kenya, Uganda, Tanzania, Zanzibar, Egypt, Ethiopia, Sudan, Malawi, Zambia, Zimbabwe, Mozambique, Angola, Madagascar and Mauritius. Part of my work was to help churches start literacy programs so that people would be able to read the Bible with understanding. If people cannot read, they cannot read God's Word. Thousands of people came to know the Lord and churches were started in remote areas through the literacy ministry. As one Kenyan woman said, "The literacy teacher built a bridge between her heart and mine and Jesus walked across that bridge into my heart." Part of my work was to help African writers prepare biblical texts in their own languages. These biblical texts were printed in more than 150 languages and millions were used in government schools and in church-sponsored literacy programs. This is my legacy to the African Church. Yes, all God's children need traveling shoes.

Recognizing that the majority of non-literates could not be reached with a printed text, I also initiated an audio scripture program with assistance from Hosanna Ministries who recorded Bibles and New Testaments in African languages and donated solar-powered tape players to enable people in the most remote areas to hear the Word of God. In 1984, I was licensed as an evangelist by the Church of God in Christ and I continued traveling even to countries outside Africa, including: Korea, Japan, Thailand, Philippines, England, France, Italy, Germany, Norway, Netherlands, Denmark, Greece, Crete, Australia and Brazil to spread the good tidings. At that time, I also asked to serve as UBS representative to the United Nations Collective Consultation on Literacy and Education for All.

When my husband, Dr. John Odhiambo Reggy passed away in 1995, I remained in Kenya. That year, the Lord led me to write a book, *Widows: the Challenges and the Choices,* to shed light on some cultural practices that are oppressive to widows in Africa. This book helped me to deal with my own loss and it opened up opportunities for me to help widows who are often marginalized and downtrodden in some countries. In 1997, I got married again to an Ethiopian educator, Mr. Kebede Mamo and in 2004 we relocated back to the USA and are now on the faculty at Beulah Heights University in Atlanta, Georgia. We teach a cross-cultural communication course. This is a good fit for our background and experience. Through this course (and speaking to mission teams in churches), the Lord has used us to train those who minister cross-culturally both at home and abroad. I also serve as Adult Education Director at Total Grace

Christian Center (TGCC) in Decatur, Georgia.

Many people ask me if I regret having spent most of my adult years in Africa. Not at all! As Maya Angelou said in her autobiography, *All God's Children Need Traveling Shoes,* her travels in Africa began a soul-searching journey that established Africa as the home of her ancestors, who generations earlier, were sold into slavery in a strange land across the ocean. For me, traveling around Africa established God's purpose for my life. Even in my older years, I am still traveling and I thank God that my children, all of whom were raised in Africa, are now traveling and making a difference too. The first daughter (a pediatrician) traveled to East Africa to do research on malaria, a major killer of children in Africa. The second daughter (an attorney) recently traveled to Jordan to train women business leaders. The third daughter (a human rights activist) is now in Rwanda doing research on the role of women in the reconciliation movement. The fourth daughter (an engineer) serves on the mission team in her church and recently traveled to Puerto Rico to share Christ with young people there. Even my grandson, age 7, has started going on mission trips. Yes, all God's children need traveling shoes. As long as the Lord gives me good health, I will continue traveling. And if a time comes when I have to take off my traveling shoes, I still want to intercede for the nations so that every person on earth will know Him.

Mae Alice Reggy-Mamo teaches at Beulah Heights University. She has a B.A. from Douglass College, Rutgers University, an M.A. from Howard University and a Ph.D. from the University of Maryland. She authored *Widows: the Challenges and the Choices* (1999) and contributed to *The Women's Study New Testament* (1995) and the *Africa Bible Commentary* (2006).

Hush! Somebody's Calling My Name
Betty Glover Palmer

"The Lord came and stood there calling as at other times, Samuel! Samuel! Then Samuel said, speak, for your servant is listening."
I Samuel 3:10.

The summer of 1988 will forever remain in the reservoir of my mind. It was a busy and exciting time for me, bringing closure to my graduate degree work in Urban Economic Development at Eastern University (formerly Eastern College). And yes, it was time to bring closure to a rewarding ten-year career at Hahnemann University, a career that had propelled my professional growth under the leadership of Dr. George Spivack. It was time to move to Atlanta, Georgia.

I was so sure that God had a purpose for me in Atlanta, Georgia. When I announced to family and friends that I would be moving to Atlanta, some thought I was tripping! Why would I leave a good job, Family, and friends and step into the unknown? My mother tried to talk me out of leaving Philadelphia, as this was the place where I had lived for more than 20 years and where my mother and siblings still lived at that time. Despite the persistence of my mother and brother, I did not waiver from what I sensed I must do. Yes, this was a tough call. Leaving behind my daughter, Monica, who would soon leave to attend Long Island University in Brooklyn, New York, was heart wrenching.

Okay, a bit of celebration was in order. A lovely farewell party was held in my honor by friends and family at my beloved Afro American Historical and Cultural Museum, where I served as a docent for many years – a perfect setting to share wonderful memories. Another celebration, a reception was given by my family church where I served in several capacities for more than 20 years. And lastly, a small intimate family gathering was hosted by my sister, Ruby. Yes, it was a time of wonderful reflections and anticipation of the journey ahead of me.

Then came that bittersweet moment when I had to say goodbye to family and friends. With ambivalence, yet with a sense of purpose, I set out for Atlanta on August 8, 1988. The transition was in motion – leaving behind my loving community of family and friends in Philadelphia. It was a hot sultry Monday morning when I hugged my mother and said goodbye. As I walked off the sun porch and down the sidewalk and tearfully joined a girl friend who was accompanying me on the drive to Atlanta, I felt butterflies in my stomach. "Hush! Somebody is calling my name."

Finally we arrived. Gratefully, I found that my apartment was intact; furniture was in place, thanks to the efforts of my brother, nephews and a good friend. I spent a couple of weeks unwinding and exploring my new community. Soon it was time to begin a new chapter in my life, beginning an internship at Greenforest Community Baptist Church, one of Dekalb County's leading churches. On August 27, 1988, energized and excited, I arrived at Greenforest Community Baptist Church in Decatur, GA., warmly greeted by Pastor George O. McCalep, Jr. and staff. I quietly observed the relaxed atmosphere throughout the facility. The facility was not the traditional church architecture structure; it was more like a school building! After settling into my small, shared office, the internship began. It consisted of organizing an employment service and conducting a feasibility study for starting a Christian school.

After the first few weeks, the excitement began to fizzle. I was missing my family, friends, familiar territories and foods I enjoyed. This was strange land for me – so much green space, no sidewalks, no urban density. Yet, the environment stirred up memories of my early days – growing up on a large farm in Jeffersonville, Georgia with my parents and 14 siblings. Ah –memories, memories, how they help us to endure the present!

The employment project went well. With the assistance of volunteers, we established a job readiness and placement program. The feasibility study was more intense, for it would determine the church's readiness to start a Christian school. Upon completion of the feasibility study, research revealed that it was not feasible to begin a school. Pastor McCalep defied the research and was guided by the Holy Spirit. He convinced the leadership to move forward with the school.

Saturday morning, January 21, 1989 was a cold cloudy day and it began as an ordinary day as I relaxed with my favorite easy listening jazz. Then I received a phone call that would make it an extraordinary day. Pastor McCalep called and stated that the leadership wanted me to serve as interim school administrator and organize Greenforest Christian Academy. I quickly asked myself, "Can I do this?" Hesitantly, I said yes. And in the next breath, Pastor McCalep dropped the bomb. We have very little money to pay you but we need you to help us make a difference in the lives of our children. Ah – what a set up! But I accepted the call as interim administrator of Greenforest Christian Academy. Surely God had called my name. I moved forward with ambition, confidence and faith.

A group of extraordinary talented and gifted persons established and served on the Board of Directors and the planning began. Weeks later the recruitment process for an administrator began. The applications flowed into the office, but not mine! When Rev. McCalep asked, "Where is your application?" I quickly responded, "I am not interested. The position does not pay enough." Really, in my heart of hearts, I doubted if I could successfully undertake that awesome responsibility. And, yes the enemy "fear of failure" raised its ugly head. Soon that excuse was eliminated when the personnel committee decided to offer me what I thought was fair compensation. Finally, I accepted the position and became the founding administrator of Greenforest Christian Academy. The Lord

64

placed the right people in place to support me. Pastor McCalep's vision was in motion. "Hush! Somebody is calling my name."

The days were long and filled with incredible hard work. I learned a new work ethic, from sun-up-to-sun-down. Saturday and Sunday could be negotiable! Both the rewards and challenges were high.

At last the morning came. Monday morning, August 21, 1989, was southern hot but was filled with excitement. A small group of dedicated teachers, directors, my administrative assistant and I gathered in the faculty lounge to pray and encourage each other as we launched the opening of Greenforest Christian Academy. Excited parents and children were greeted and welcomed with open arms. Our hearts received 75 anxious students in grades K4 through 7th grade and 35 preschoolers. History was in the making!

Today, that school is known as, Greenforest McCalep Christian Academic Center and has an enrollment of nearly 800 students, ranging from preschool through twelfth grade. Look at God in action!

Ecclesiastes 3:1 lets us know that "to every thing, there is a season and a time for every purpose under the heaven." And in September 1992, my season at Greenforest ended. I had successfully lived and written the first chapter in the history of Greenforest Christian Academy. And now the season to minister in the Atlanta inner city was upon me.

With ambivalence, I announced my resignation. It created a flurry of emotions among board members, parents and staff. I vividly recall one staff person saying to me, "I should hit you in the head for leaving your baby. How could you do this?" Another person questioned whether God was calling me to work in the inner city of Atlanta – dark places! Yes, I was sure of the call. God was in charge and I must move to his beat. "Hush! Somebody is calling my name."

I arrived at FCS Urban Ministries on a late fall morning in 1992. I was happy to join those in inner city transformation. One of Atlanta's leading community economic development organizations, FCS, an umbrella of ministries, was founded by Dr. Robert Lupton. I had been called to lead the economic development organization to the next level.   For more than six years I led FCS Community Economic Development as we provided goods, services, job training and jobs for a deserving community. It was a rewarding experience, working in the community, listening to the people and feeling their heartbeat.

My work in the community with families, leaders and pastors revealed that the church was, indeed, a catalyst for community economic development.   Yet, many pastors and leaders needed relevant skills. Again, in response to another call, I launched a new ministry that would provide economic development training and technical assistance to pastors and leaders. Today, that ministry is known as **B.G. Palmer Economic Development Training.**

Late summer 2002, another call came. I was sanctioned to Beulah Heights Bible College, now known as Beulah Heights University. For more than 90 years Beulah Heights, with a global outreach, has been preparing Christian leaders for ministry and marketplace. The college's former president, Samuel Chand, offered me a challenge to raise money to revamp the Urban Studies Department. This involved creating a new curriculum and the Institute for Urban and Global Economic Development. I thought to myself, "Oh, no…Raise money? Not again. My spirit convicted me to accept the challenge. "Hush! Somebody is calling my name."

In July 2003, we held the historical opening of the Institute for Urban and Global Community Economic Development, the only one of its kind in the nation, in a Bible College.   I was appointed Chair for the Department of Urban Studies and associate professor and currently Chair for the Leadership Studies under the leadership of Dr. Benson Karanja, president.   What a phenomenal opportunity to train leaders to transform communities. It was at Beulah Heights, where I was ordained in Para-church ministry by the Evangelical Church Alliance.

My journey has taken me full circle – from the rural farm life to the great metropolis and urban center; from the front line of delivering educational services and community development to establishing a program that trains others to become community de-velopers and transformers. What an amazing journey! Like Samuel, God has called my name. I have responded. My life has been transformed and He has used me to help others transform their lives. More importantly, I have been obedient to God's call. What I know for sure, God calls ordinary people to do extraordinary work for Him. "Hush! Somebody's calling my name."

Betty Glover Palmer is an amazing woman of God who continues to blaze trails. She currently serves as professor and Chair for the Department of Leadership Studies at Beulah Heights University in Atlanta, Georgia. A passionate advocate for community economic development, she has been recognized by Eastern University as an accomplished alumnus in the field. She holds a Master's degree in Urban Economic Development from Eastern University and is certified in Faith-based Community Economic Development through the Harvard University Divinity School Summer Leadership Program. She is the mother of one daughter and grandmother of two grandchildren.

I've Come This Far By Faith
Dee Thornton

"Now faith is the substance of things hoped for, the evidence of things not seen." Hebrew 11:1

My life's journey has seen many twists and turns, i.e., great times, good times and some not so wonderful times. However, I would just like to share one very small slice of my journey for your consideration. (Because of my Messianic faith, I have excluded the "o" from God.)

One of my heart's desires when I was a younger woman was to have a loving husband and many children. I didn't particularly care about college at that point in my life; but I just wanted to be loved by a wonderful man. However, I ended up with several counterfeits, and in the process I missed the hand of G-d over and over again. My eyes and my heart were so filled with my own desires, that somehow I couldn't see what G-d was plainly displaying to me all along. Yet, in spite of some of my regrets, and my own blindness, G-d's hand was always on my life. His grace was there even though I was unaware of His providence or chose to ignore His will.

I was legally joined to the same man for 21 years, and in that time we experienced many things as a family; some fine times and some ugly times. We lost beloved family members, we lost a child together, we lost property, our youngest son suffered from various health issues, our middle child suffered some abuse and our oldest boy seemed carefree. Conversely, we traveled, partied, entertained often, and acquired some wonderful possessions, and I obtained a teaching credential. Yet, through all the aforementioned events true intimacy and consequently, respect, seemed to always be missing. Let me explain.

As a young woman, this wonderful man I dreamed about was not only an excellent husband and father, but also a very dear friend. This someone, whom I adored and liked according to my dream, would also feel the same about me. Yet, in the real world of that marriage, intimacy beyond the sheets was not the center piece in our relationship and neither was G-d. G-d had never sanctioned the marriage, but He did show up and revealed Himself in many ways through the course of the marriage. In fact, (retrospectively), G-d revealed His stop sign or "do not pass go sign" prior to the wedding. I chose to ignore those signs, for I knew that love would make all things right. As the story of that particular slice of my journey unfolded, it became evident that G-d was right all along, and divorce ensued many years later.

However, in looking back, I realize that I didn't have an intimate relationship with the Father, and so the signs of G-d were explained away. Yet, as the marriage was beginning to consistently go downhill, I realized that I had replaced the living G-d with my children's biological father. Therefore, G-d was never the author of our marriage; nor had He joined us together. Hence, I remained in an unhappy marriage and an emotionally abusive situation far too long, at the expense of my children and myself. Yet, G-d in His mercy and kindness never abandoned me. He not only kept me safe and sane, but He also kept the entire family safe. He miraculously managed my son's illness and He provided for our needs.

Now in all fairness, I was the one who did most of the changing and realized who I married was more of a figment of my imagination. I was mesmerized by his great looks, personality, charm and sex appeal, as well as his doting attention in the beginning of the marriage. However, as the years rolled by, and the children came, the dream became a nightmare and it seemed as if I was losing myself, in that my self-esteem was extremely low. You may ask, "Why did you stay so long?" There are many reasons --- more than I am willing to divulge --- but in a nutshell, it was for the sake of the marriage and the children. I never wanted a divorce, and I did not want my children to be without their dad.

The details of the things which led to the eventual destruction are of no consequence because the main idea is that G-d was always there whether I realized it or not. We both played a major role in the demise of our relationship and we both have suffered consequences for our choice. Through all the events of that particular relationship, I learned many things about G-d, myself and others. I learned that G-d can heal a broken heart and soothe a wounded soul if we allow Him to have His way. I learned that no man (or woman) can take the place of a loving heavenly Father, as He is the only one who can give us what our hearts really desire. I learned that only through forgiveness can I truly be free. I learned that only in Messiah do I have self-worth and receive the strength to do what is required to provide for children and self. I learned that no one can love me like the L-rd. I learned that sex clouds and blinds our thinking when we are getting to know a person. I learned that next to G-d, a loving mother is the next best thing. I learned that G-d always knows best, and that His teachings and ways which seem hard are for our good! Finally, I learned that G-d loved me so very much that He sent Messiah to die for my sins, and then He called me to serve and share His goodness with others.

In closing, G-d really does use all things for the good for those who love Him, as I am a living testimony of G-d's goodness and His continued restoring and nurturing of my soul. Therefore, as I move forward in the things of Messiah, my prayer is that I continue to remember the old lessons and embrace the new lessons so that my living is a loving, holy testimony pleasing before G-d.

The "o" is missing from G-d and L-rd as a sign of respect and honor, for He is the Most Holy G-d, The One true One, the Creator and Sustainer of the universe. By leaving out the "o" it makes the distinction that this author is not speaking of an idol, which uses the name "god", but is referring to the One true G-d who revealed

Himself to Moses as the I AM. Further, it is considered by many as one of the ways to fulfill the first mitzvah (commandment) which tells us that we are not to take the L-rd's name in vain. Shalom! Pastor Dee Thornton

---

Pastor Dee Thornton co-pastors Yeshua's Messianic Community, Inc. in Stone Mountain, Georgia. Pastor Dee taught third grade at Greenforest Christian Academy and is currently a reading recovery teacher within the Gwinnett County educational system. She has a B.A. from National University; a Master's of Divinity and is currently seeking to begin a Ph.D. program through Trinity College of the Bible Theological Seminary, located in Newburgh, Indiana.

The Journey of a Purpose Driven Teacher
Martha Sanogo Amponsah

"Now, in all these things we are more than conquerors through Him who loved us." ~ Romans 8:37.

    Little did I realize over 15 years ago when I decided to pursue a graduate degree in Education that I was not only pursing a career in teaching, but actually embarking upon a profound ministry.

    This became evident to me when I did my graduate internship at the juvenile detention center. My professor told the class that we would spend our summer setting up a summer program for the youth at the detention center. We were told to write a unit and lesson plans for ten weeks on the subject that we intended to teach. Our target audience age ranged from 11-years-old to 16-years-old.

    My initial thought was one of panic. The jail? Criminals? What would I teach? The Holy Spirit immediately convicted me and I heard these words, *"They are only children and you will teach them the same way you would teach your very own children."* I spent the next couple of days planning, purchasing, and researching with enthusiasm and excitement.

    When I entered the jail on the first day of my internship, I was again gripped with panic and fear. However, it was short-lived.

Once I witnessed the hopeless eyes of my young brothers, I realized that this was an opportunity for me to be a "vessel of change" in their lives. A quote from one of my favorite ministers is, "I am anointed to change the atmosphere." Well, this was my sentiment exactly. I felt as if I was anointed and appointed to change the atmosphere. Everyday, as I entered that juvenile facility, my prayers were, "Let me impact in some small way the lives of everyone I meet."

However, my life was definitely impacted when I began to interact with real people with unfortunate stories. Sometimes as humans we are quick to judge others without knowing the entire situation. I heard stories about the harsh realities that life had dealt some of the young brothers. For example, parents using crack cocaine, abusive parents or family members, and a history of career criminals as role models were what many experienced. There were 16-year-olds that could not read or write. Whose fault was this? Where did the blame lie? I didn't have the time to concern myself with these matters. My only concern was to desperately try to make a difference. When I told them how special they were and that they were created to do wonderful things in this world, they looked at me with total disbelief. Their eyes asked, "Is this true?," "Can I trust her," and "Does she really believe this?" It has been said that our eyes are the windows of our souls, and their eyes spoke to me in a very powerful way. After weeks of teaching and encouraging the students, some of them began to warm up and ask for help. Some of them asked me to help them learn to read and write, while others asked for prayer. I may never know, but perhaps, just perhaps, a seed was planted in some of their lives. I was told by one of the students that next to their one male classmate, I knew how to relate to him.

Today, I find myself on the other end of the spectrum. I now have the opportunity and privilege of working with very young children. Some have been labeled "special needs" but they all believe and know that they are unique and special. They are untainted by life's blows, scars, rejection and pain. When you tell them that they are unique and special, their little eyes say, "I know it and if you say it, you must believe it, too." They are ready to embrace life with a positive, optimistic attitude and become all that they can become because someone believes in them.

When I go to work each day I think about my personal situation. I carry in my bosom the thoughts of my daughter. My daily prayers are, "God, please send _real_ teachers across her path today. Please send someone today who will look beyond her outside appearances and see her heart. Please send someone who will encourage and motivate her to be all that **You** have created her to be." You see, I realize that a teacher may come in the form of a bus driver, coach, cafeteria worker, school secretary or another parent.

One day God sent a wonderful teacher into my life. That person was Dr. Regina Anderson. Dr. Anderson has an innate ability to draw out of peoples' abilities that they never knew existed. My first encounter with Dr. Anderson was when she came to our school as our new principal. She began to make requests that my co-workers and I felt were totally unrealistic and out of our range.

During our plight of bewilderment, she spoke words of encouragement to her staff and empowered us to rise to the next level. Eventually, we began to fly and not only fly, but to soar to new heights unknown to us or our school. Her gentle, persistent spirit ignited inner potentials deep from inside every one of us. Dr. Anderson's deep compassion and love for people serves as a healing balm that repairs and propels.

Dr. Anderson's spiritual giftedness helped me to recognize talents that had lain dormant for years. I personally credit her for where I am today, both spiritually and emotionally. You see, three years ago I wanted to give up and walk away from my calling. I had become totally consumed by life's disappointments. Ironically, I never voiced these sentiments to anyone. Nevertheless, being the woman of God that she is, "she knew." When I was so devastated and couldn't pray for myself, she prayed for me. She fought for me when I refused to fight for myself because I felt so unworthy. Today, I am eternally grateful to her for touching my life and not giving up on me. She taught me a powerful lesson. As an Elder, she taught me my history. She taught me that people of African descent have always embodied with a strong sense of family and community.

Historically, we cared about each other and were very supportive of each other. That was all we knew. If it happened to you, it happened to me. Because you are, I am. It is now my personal obligation to extend this life's lesson on to others. Because she showed me compassion and love, I can and must extend it on.

So remember that ministers are not merely the men or women standing in the pulpit. Ministry is a form of teaching and we are all teachers in our own unique way. When we consciously or unconsciously decide to positively change the atmosphere, we are teaching by example. Remember, more lessons are caught than taught. When you show someone love, concern, caring, understanding, encouragement and motivation, you are exercising a teaching ministry. When you take time to touch someone's life with a thought, a word or a deed, you are achieving the ultimate ministry... teaching. Proverbs 16:22 and 24 says, "Understanding is a wellspring of life to him who has it and pleasant words are like a honeycomb, sweetness to the soul and health to the bones." We all have the power and capacity to make a difference in someone's life. ***Who have you taught today***? You never know who is waiting to hear from you.

Mrs. Martha Sanogo Amponsah holds a B.A. degree in Sociology from St. Leo University and an M.A. degree in Education from Clark Atlanta University. She is an educator, entrepreneur, wife and mother. She enjoys cooking, reading, writing, shopping, traveling and spending quality time with her family and friends. Mrs. Amponsah's future goals include pursuing her Ph.D. and writing children's books.

You Shall Live and Not Die

Ain't Got Time to Die
Joy L. Coffey

"Even though I walk through the valley of the shadow of death, I will fear no evil, for you are with me; your rod and your staff, they comfort me." ~ Psalm 23:4

> *Lord, I keep so busy praisin' my Jesus*
> *Keep so busy praisin' my Jesus*
> *Keep so busy praisin' my Jesus*
> *Ain't got time to die.*

My life was going just great! . . . just got engaged to get married and moved into a lovely home. I really felt that I was on the right track with accomplishing the goals that I had prayed for and set out to achieve. My family had always been very proud of my accomplishments in life and was very supportive in my endeavors. Everything seemed to be moving right along.

One morning as I was preparing for work, I looked in the mirror and was not happy with what I saw. My zeal and sparkle, which I had always noticed about myself, was not reflecting back to me in the mirror. I thought to myself, "There is something wrong with this picture." Not knowing what was wrong with my body; I talked to a close friend and shared my symptoms. She convinced me to schedule a doctor's appointment immediately. Without hesitation, I scheduled an appointment to see my doctor.

While sitting in the lobby of the doctor's office, I began to ponder over what was really going on with my body. I always felt that I was in good health. I knew that I had procrastinated with setting up appointments and would often put my family's needs before my own health issues. As I was deep in thought, I heard the nurse call my name and she proceeded to take me back to a medical screening room. Once the nurse had taken my vital signs, her face seemed quite perplexed and alarming. I asked her what was the matter and her response to me was, "Just a moment; I must get the doctor to come and see you immediately."

Now I am not one to get concerned immediately, but her response caused me to question in my mind, "What is really wrong?"

At the time of my medical appointment, my parents were out of town for a few days and here I was in the doctor's office all by myself.

The doctor finally came in to examine me. He began asking me a lot of questions regarding my health for the past month. I mentioned to him jokingly that I was frequently using the restroom – more often than usual for a person of my age – and my sleeping pattern was off. He asked me about my family medical history. I mentioned to him that both of my parents had high blood pressure. I told him that my previous doctor had placed me on high blood pressure medications for a limited time. The doctor then informed me that my blood pressure was 210/120, which was extremely high, and I was very close to having a stroke. When the doctor said that I was close to having a stroke, it took a moment for his words to set into my mind. "What could have happened," I thought. Calmly, he indicated that I had to stay at the clinic in a holding room until my pressure came down. So here I was with this dilemma staring me right in the face.

After resting in the holding room, which seemed to be forever and my pressure was at a point of normalcy, the doctor allowed me to go home. His medical instructions to me were bed rest, not to over exert myself and to come back to see him the next day. He wanted to monitor my blood pressure for the week. I called my parents to inform them about what had happened. My mother asked, "Are you going to follow the doctor's instructions?" My response to her was "Yes, I am."

After the third day of visitation to the doctor, my blood pressure had not come down. This was not the medical result that my doctor wanted to see. He informed me that he wanted to have more tests done and additional medical consultation, so he was going to admit me into the hospital. This was shocking news to me. What medical diagnosis was the doctor searching for? When I left home, I had no reason to think that this was going to happen. I became frightened because my immediate family was out of town. At that moment, I felt all alone. "What am I going to do?" I wondered. Then I began to pray and the 23rd Psalm came to mind:

"The Lord is my shepherd, I shall not want. He maketh me to lie down in green pastures. He leadeth me beside the still waters. He restoreth my soul. He leadeth me in the paths of righteousness for his name's sake. Yea, though I walk through the valley of the shadow of death, I will fear no evil, for thou art with me; thy rod and thy staff they will comfort me. Thou preparest a table before me in the presence of my enemies; thou anointest my head with oil; my cup runneth over. Surely goodness and mercy shall follow me all the days of my life and I will dwell in the house of the Lord forever." (KJV)

After repeating the 23rd Psalm, calmness came over me and I knew everything would be alright because God controls everything in our lives.

I called my cousin who came to support me while my parents returned home. My mother was very worried and I reassured her that everything would be alright because God was in control. The doctor ordered several tests to be completed and finally my blood pressure came down to his satisfaction. After receiving the results from the test, the doctor explained to my family what was going on physically with my body. I was in the beginning stage of renal failure.

Renal failure! How could this be! I did not know what this medical diagnosis meant. The doctor explained that my kidneys were not functioning properly and I had to begin dialysis treatment. I was scheduled to have surgery to prepare my left arm for the needles that would have to be inserted into my arm for treatment. Everything was happening so quickly and I had no clue about the procedure for dialysis; but God knows what you need and how to prepare individuals to be a beacon of hope and support when the time arises.

At my local church, a support group met monthly to discuss medical concerns and issues for individuals who had medical challenges such as renal failure, lupus or diabetes. This group was birthed and founded by Rev. Jay Wilson. Rev. Jay was an individual who had experienced and lived the life of renal failure. I felt like a small child learning how to take baby steps, as I began learning about my illness – renal failure. Rev. Jay always made our sessions about renal failure educational and everything was spiritually connected. Rev. Jay always reminded the group that their illness was a "condition" that could be controlled with proper physical and mental habits. I was able to renew my strength and self-esteem by being a part of the support group. No longer did I feel lifeless. I began to look at life through another lens. I began to ask myself, "What is God trying to say to you or show you? Are you going to sink in the whirlpool of pity or are you going to become a beacon of strength for others?"

I began treatment during the summer months and adjusted to my new way of living. Praise God, I was able to continue to work and my family and friends did everything to support me. As I learned more about renal failure by attending seminars and workshops, I began to meet young Christian women who were experiencing the same condition. We developed a strong bond and were supportive of each other.

It was at a workshop where I encountered the miraculous works of the Holy Spirit. I was gathering some information about additional health services for renal patients. As I was reading the young woman who was at the booth approached me and said that God had just revealed to her that my blessing was on its way this very moment and to receive it when it came. I looked at her strangely but responded by saying, "I receive it." I left and continued to participate in the workshop. About 45 minutes later, I received a phone call indicating that I had received a donor for a transplant. Look at God and how He works through many different channels of people.

I was blessed to have the transplanted kidney for three years. During that time, I was able to return to a normal way of living, but I still had health concerns and a restricted diet. I learned how to adjust and move on with life. Although I've had to return back to dialysis treatments I still live life to the fullest and thank God each day for the blessing of life.

Lord, I keep so busy praisin' my Jesus
Keep so busy praisin' my Jesus
Keep so busy praisin' my Jesus
Ain't got time to die.

Joy L. Coffey is a native of New Orleans, La. currently residing in Atlanta, Georgia. She is a graduate of Tuskegee University in Tuskegee, Alabama and Clark Atlanta University in Atlanta, Georgia. She is employed with the Atlanta Public Schools System as a guidance counselor. She has been a dialysis patient for nine years and is an active member of the Dialysis Transplantation Support Ministry at her church, Greenforest Community Baptist Church in Decatur, Georgia.

I'm So Glad Trouble Don't Last Always
Millie Green-Hebert

"But the salvation of the righteous is from the LORD; He is their strength in the time of trouble." ~ Psalm 37:39

I wouldn't take nothing for my journey in spite of the hills and valleys that I have experienced. In March of this year I experienced so much joy when my first great-grandchild, Fabiane, was born healthy, happy and beautiful at 8 pounds and 11 ounces. I had not finished thanking God for this little blessing when everything changed.

My younger daughter, who is 45-years-old, went in for her routine mammogram, which was abnormal. A repeat mammogram followed an ultrasound and then a biopsy. Yes, she had breast cancer. I don't think that I have ever prayed so hard in my life as I did during these few weeks. At the same time I began experiencing severe abdominal pain near the site of the surgical scar from a left Nephrectomy; I had kidney cancer in 1994. My physician ordered a series of diagnostic tests, which showed that I had a thickening of the colon and a spot on my liver. By this time I was so stressed I could not think clearly and was having memory problems. I was on automatic pilot. I prayed and prayed for God to let me have cancer instead of my daughter.

My pastor asked me to read Psalm 103 out loud three times a day and I am still doing this at this time. I also recited my favorite Bible verse all during the day, "I can do all things through Christ who strengthens me." There were times when I couldn't pray and I would say, "Jesus, Jesus," over and over again. I cancelled my trip to St. Louis to visit an old friend who has Parkinson's and confronted my valley experience with all of the strength that I had, depending on God to see me through.

I am still going through this valley experience holding on to my faith and prayers with the assurance that we will get through the struggles and there are brighter days ahead. My daughter had a lumpectomy. There was no metastasis and the tumor was small and she is doing well physically and emotionally. She will not need chemotherapy but will start radiation next week and after that she will take Tamoxifen. No malignancy has been found during my testing so far.

My daily prayer is, "Thank you God, thank you Jesus." I feel that my family and I are not traveling this journey alone. We know with God's assurance that Trouble Don't Last Always.

Millie Green- Herbert is a graduate of Florida A & M University in Nurse Education. A retired coordinator of School Nursing, she has traveled extensively as a military family. She is the mother of five children, five grandchildren and one great-grandchild.

They Said I Wouldn't Make It ...But I Did
Rev. Paula Christian Stallworth

"But as for you, you meant evil against me; but God meant it for good, in order to bring it about as it is this day, to save many people alive." ~ *Genesis 50:20*

Much of the information I am about to share is nothing to be proud of. I am not telling the story so that you will think I am great or have done great things. I share so that you will know that no matter what "they" may have said about you in your life, "they" could be lying. The naysayers who said I would not make it were wrong. When I learned as a young woman that there were those who not only said I wouldn't make it, but told everyone in the family, I made up my mind to show them. I decided to make sure that their prophecy did not come to pass. Had I continued in the direction I was headed, my story's ending would, however, be different.

When people were saying I would never make it, I would have to agree that it looked that way. I was a rebellious teen who was angry at the world. After my parents separated and divorced, I went ballistic. I fought every person --- man, woman or peer --- who irritated me. My first fight was with my third grade teacher. One warm spring day when she announced that it was time for recess, I resisted. When she tried to force me, the "battle" began. She hit me

84

with the ruler; I hit her back. I stomped on her foot and bit her. That was the first of several fights I had with her.

I began to live my life on the edge. I joined a gang and hung out in West Philadelphia. Some of my peers were killed as a result of gang banging, but somehow, I made it. Twice when hospitalized the doctor told me I almost did not make it. On another occasion when hanging out, I was approached by a strange man who told me that if I did not leave the club with him he would drag me out. Another night, while I was waiting for the bus to go home after work, a man came behind me, put a screwdriver to my neck and said if I screamed he would stab me and throw me in the bushes. These are just a few of the many times God spared my life.

... But They Lied

I am now a middle-aged professional African American woman who is currently pursuing a doctorate degree. I am a licensed counselor, certified as an addictions' counselor, and am building a private practice called The Listening Ear. My motto is *"Listening when others won't, hearing when others can't.* I am employed as the director of a resource center in prevention services. My work allows me to impact students K-12, churches, organizations, agencies, city and local government systems, colleges, universities and other professionals. I serve on two boards, three coalitions and a panel review committee as an advocate for children for a local juvenile court system. My second place of employment is with a youth development center where I am a substance abuse counselor four nights per week.

I, along with a team of 12 people, planted The Potter's House Christian Church and Ministries, Inc., "A Place to Begin Again," in 1994. Today, The Potter's House is working hard D.W.J.D. (Doing What Jesus Did) ministering to the POW's i.e., poor, oppressed, orphans and widows. I am a charter member of an organization called Sisters on the Journey. Yes, I am on a journey and what a wonderful journey it has turned out to be. Last year my sister, our husbands and I spent our birthdays in Europe. Today, I am married (17 years) and together we have three successful adult sons who have given us seven wonderful grandchildren.

There are many days I wish I could do some things over. I have caused many people much pain, especially my children. I have asked their forgiveness and I strive everyday to thrive in the things of God Almighty for being so good to me and even better, for me. I thank my God every day for the grace afforded my children and me.

When I came to myself in 1979, I went back to the church and rededicated my life to Christ. Not long after that, a gospel song came out by Luther Barnes and the Red Bud Choir entitled, "They Said I Wouldn't Make It." Those words speak volumes to my story. "They said I wouldn't make it. They said I wouldn't be here today. They said I wouldn't amount to anything. But I'm glad to say, that I am on my way and growing more and more each day."

Rev. Paula Christian Stallworth serves as solo pastor of The Potter's House Christian Ministries, Inc. in metro Atlanta, Georgia. She is a native of New Rochelle, New York. She graduated from Beulah Heights Bible College Magna Cum Laude in 1997. She has a Master's of Divinity in Christian Education and Pastoral Care Counseling from the Interdenominational Theological Center in Atlanta, Georgia.

Reflections and Praise
LaVergne White

"I will bless the Lord at all times: His praise shall continually be in my mouth." ~ Psalm 34:1

As I reflect over being trapped in my home as Hurricane Katrina approached New Orleans that Sunday through Wednesday in August 2005, one thought was with me at all times, "In everything give praise, for this is the will of God" (I Thessalonians 5:18). At that time, there was about three to four feet of water in my house. I had four candles, a flash light, bottled water, corn flakes, canned goods such as carrots and string beans. No electricity, no telephone. I was unable to communicate. Had I stepped off of my porch, the water would have been over my head.

I am so happy that I have a deep relationship with God. As I waded through the water in my home, I asked God to surround me with His loving arms of protection. Each morning I would wade to the piano and play and sing:

> "I love you Lord, and I lift my voice
> to worship you, oh my soul rejoices.
> Take joy my king in what you hear,
> may it be a sweet, sweet sound in
> your ear."

I had a schedule: bathe in the kitchen sink, worship and praise at the piano, eat corn flakes and drink water, take the tape recorder on the porch, sit on the stool to my organ and play religious tapes, eat lunch of carrots or string beans and prayer, and see how many candles I had left. Often I waved to the helicopters with a white towel so that they would know I was there. At night I would wet my clothing all over so I could be reasonably cool. Then I would pray and try to get some sleep while the things in the house floated all through the night making weird noises.

Over and over again I checked the water outside my kitchen window and on the front. It was not going down. I told the Lord Wednesday morning, "Lord I am still praising you and waiting for you to rescue me. I know you don't seem to be moving as I desire, but I know you will be on time."

Many thoughts went through my mind at the time. I was 75-years-young, Insulin dependent, diabetic, overweight, short winded but happy - happy that I was alive! You probably are wondering how I could have been happy. Well, Jesus never fails. I just knew He was making a way for me and He did. A boat came and got me from my house. When I was in the water, my prayer was, "Lord, I praise you as my deliverer and that you will deliver me from this water." I ended up in the Houston, Texas Astrodome. I called my daughters' cell phones and they too had stopped in Houston. However, they left New Orleans that Sunday at 5:00 a.m. When I called them they were hysterical. They thought I had drowned. My daughters came to the Astrodome that Thursday and picked me up.

Remember, when you go through rough times, cling to God, refuse to let your doubts or fears silence your praise and you will see how God sustains you. It doesn't matter how terrible or difficult your situation is; every time you praise God He will move into the situation to redeem and transform it in some way.

Even though loss, disappointments or failures can be crippling, don't allow your faith in the goodness of God and His love to wavier. His promise is that, "All things work together for the good…" (Romans 8:28). That means that something good will come out of even your greatest tragedy. Although I lost my home and everything I owned, God's love, grace and mercy assures us that

88

even though we endure deep sorrow, "Joy comes in the morning" (Psalm 30:5).

Presently, I am living in Silver Spring, Maryland in a Senior Citizen complex. Each week I minister to the other residents; I have a Gospel hour. We sing, read scriptures and poetry, and I speak briefly on various subjects about God's goodness. My daily prayer is, "Father, let your love pour through me to all who listen."

When you go through difficult times, remember who sustains you. Remember who led you there. He is Lord of the mountains, as well as the valley. So no matter where you find yourself, praise God for all His worth. Praising God will change your life!

As I consider my experiences in life, I embrace them all for whatever I have learned from them. I am now 79-years-young and still on the journey!

LaVergne White is a native of New Orleans, Louisiana. She is a graduate of Dillard University, an accomplished musician, instructor, choir director and retired director of Treme Head Start. The Katrina victim is now living on the east coast.

This Little Light of Mine
Paula Smith Broadnax

". . . let your light shine before men, that they may see your good deeds and praise your Father in heaven." ~ Matthew 5:16

This little light of mine; I'm going to let it shine; Oh, this little light of mine; I'm going to let it shine; Hallelujah; This little light of mine; I'm going to let it shine; Let it shine; let it shine; let it shine.

Ev'ry where I go; I'm going to let it shine; Oh, ev'ry where I go; I'm going to let it shine; Hallelujah; Ev'ry where I go; I'm going to let it shine; Let it shine; let it shine; let it shine.

All in my house; I'm going to let it shine; Oh, all in my house; I'm going to let it shine; Hallelujah; All in my house; I'm going to let it shine; Let it shine; let it shine; let it shine.

During December 2007 one of my spiritual advisors preached a series of sermons that dared us to move forward with what God had planted in our minds to do. For me, that meant to write my story of how I had lived my dream! He challenged us by saying don't be afraid to DREAM or have a vision. He said there is HOPE in a dream but our dream must be Christ-centered and driven by a passion to make a difference in the lives of others. He further encouraged us to dream of the POSSIBILITIES. In the series of sermons he admonished us to "tell our God story." This is my desire . . . to let others know that "all things are possible to those who love the Lord." He told us that God hears and answers prayers. My story is that of an answered prayer fulfilled in part by so many people who were praying for and with me. And finally, he reminded us that wise men and women continue to seek God.

I believe that what I have to share will encourage others to move forward with the dreams God has given to them. I believe my story will help others to not be afraid to "Let your light so shine; before men, that they may see your good works, and glorify your Father which is in heaven" (KJV Matthew 5:16) and to ". . . write the vision; make it plain . . ." (Habakkuk: 2:3) because when God gives the vision, He will also give the provision. Seek God continually and move forward knowing that if you take one step, He'll take two! Seek opportunities to share with others all along the way how God is blessing you to be able to work toward the dream He has given. And remember, where there are DREAMS there is HOPE and where there is HOPE there are POSSIBILITIES!

I have found one of my spiritual gifts is hospitality and I recently came across a definition that truly describes what I believe hospitality is: **"Hospitality is not just an event; it is a lifestyle intended to point others to God's family."** Several years ago a church sister and dear friend of mine and I decided to combine our dreams. Her dream was to live on an island and mine was to own a bed and breakfast inn in the Caribbean. After much prayer, planning began. We became consumed with the idea and began taking classes, visiting inns, talking with innkeepers and basically doing everything we knew possible to ensure that we were successful and were giving God our best.

After being divorced for 18 years, I met a wonderful, godly gentleman whom I married five months after meeting him. He was delighted and excited about my dream. We later discovered that he was actually the missing link. You see, my dream could not have become a reality without him. (Isn't that just like God?) He had all the necessary skills and talents to ensure that the vision could be accomplished.

A year after marrying, I was diagnosed with breast cancer. Now before you say, "Oh no!" let me assure you that it was what was necessary for me to become the godly woman I am today. You see, that experience forced me to "let go and let God." It put me in a place to allow others to do for me and for me to relinquish the "Superwoman" role; and it made me fully aware of how precious and fleeting life is.

Before starting the chemo and radiation treatments, I spent some time at the monastery to meditate and pray. After my retreat, I felt ready to move forward. Upon completion of the treatments, I retired from my job with my mother's blessings (which truly meant a lot). My husband and I sold our belongings and moved to St. Croix, USVI. I had spent numerous vacations in the Caribbean and was often mistaken for someone's "cousin," so this felt like going home! Life took my friend in another direction and she went on a two-year mission assignment in Seoul, South Korea.

Inn Paradise, a five-room bed and breakfast inn overlooking the Caribbean Sea, was created. The hard work and long hours was one of the most fulfilling things I have ever done. After we began receiving guests from all over the world, it became very apparent that this was bigger than just an inn - it was a MINISTRY. Hebrews 13:1-2 tells us, "Let brotherly love continue. Be not forgetful to entertain strangers; for thereby some have entertained angels unawares."

You see, we found that when people are hurting, if you make them comfortable with you and in their environment this sets the stage for them to open up and share. What we heard from people was that life presents the same life issues and challenges regardless of where you are from. Having been recently diagnosed with cancer, I had the opportunity to share with many of our guests who were also in various stages of cancer. I believe that our sharing was healing and therapeutic to them as well as for me.

In the beginning there were periods of time when we had no guests. When rooms were empty we did not turn away people in need, like a lady found at the beach ready to commit suicide. Someone found her and brought her to us so that she could have a restful night. The next morning she went on her way, later returning to thank us for showing her so much love. After settling on the island, another one of our guests (a radiologist with the hospital) developed a problem with alcohol and found himself on the street. He came back to us and we took in him, prayed with him and counseled him to seek help. Before leaving the island, he returned to express his thanks for our concern for his well being and support.

It was a joy to host many community events such as a men's Bible study, rehearsals for the community choir, and cancer support meetings. These events lent an atmosphere of outreach and fellowship, which enriched and blessed the participants and us.

Many things began to change for us and other small business owners on St. Croix. The tragedy of 9/11 brought fewer guests because flights were removed. Many businesses closed. Tommie and I prayed for direction and concluded that this season had ended and we should return home. The big deciding factor was that we wanted to be a part of our grandchildren's lives and watch them grow up. As we were preparing to return to the states, it was bittersweet. We knew that God had just begun to do a work in us and our desire was and is to allow Him to continue to use us. One of our guests reminded us that the inn was us and not the building. As we move forward our desire is to create and live a lifestyle designed to point others to God's family. It is envisioned that one day we will create another place for people to "come aside by yourselves to a deserted place and rest for a while" (Mark 6:31).

For more, look for Paula's soon to be published book: Dreams, Hopes and Possibilities - a breast cancer survivor's story of a dream come true.

Paula Smith Broadnax is the wife of Tommie, "Grandma" Paula to 13 and a 12-year breast cancer survivor. Paula retired from a 30-year managerial career in the telecommunications industry in June 1998. This equipped her to pursue her entrepreneurial spirit. Active in the cancer ministry at her church, Paula is writing her first book detailing how she was blessed to live her dream of creating a bed and breakfast inn in the Caribbean.

Trouble Don't Last Always
Camille Turnbull-Williams

"If thou faint in the day of adversity, thy strength is small." ~
Proverbs 24: 10

It was Sunday morning, August 29, 2005. The warnings were coming about this dreadful storm approaching. Hurricane Katrina was making its way towards New Orleans! We had been through many previous hurricanes including the awful Betsy. Therefore, we were not too alarmed. Mayor Nagin was on T.V. advising the citizens of New Orleans to evacuate, but we were determined to "ride it out." We boarded up the windows; put all moveable objects away and prepared food and water for our anticipated stay. We and our neighbors agreed to go into the four-story building across the street if it became necessary. Our granddaughter and her family had evacuated the night before. She continued to call and cry, begging us to leave because she "had a terrible feeling" about this storm. (Was it the Lord speaking through her?)

We finally conceded and threw a few clothes into a suitcase – enough for two days. We assumed we would be returning to New Orleans by Wednesday. We got ready to go and realized the car had been leaking oil and we would have to keep adding oil every few miles, which would be impossible. The only other vehicle available was our old 1991 Chevy truck – but did it have gas in it? Luckily it happened that my brother had borrowed it the day before and "hallelujah" he had left the tank full!! That old ragged truck brought us all the way to our daughter's family home in Humble, Texas before it gave out completely. We lost almost all of our earthly possessions, but through the grace of God we realize that trouble really does not last always.

I'm so glad that trouble doesn't last always. We have settled in Humble, Texas and so has our entire family, including our three daughters, their husbands and five of our grandchildren and four of our eight great-grandchildren. The granddaughter who insisted that we evacuate is now living in San Antonio, Texas with her husband and their four children. We anticipate that they will soon move to Humble, Texas. I know that when I was in trouble, Jesus lifted me.

Camille Turnbull-Williams was born in New Orleans, Louisiana and educated in the Catholic schools. She graduated from Dillard University and pursued graduate studies at Clark Atlanta University. Camille was an educator for 38 years in New Orleans, Louisiana and an organist at Haven United Methodist and Brooks United Methodist Church. She also sang for 20 years in the New Orleans Black Chorale singing music by black composers.

My Soul Is a Witness
Barbara Cross

"We will not hide them from their children; we will tell the next generation the praiseworthy deeds of the LORD, his power, and the wonders he has done." ~ Psalm 78:4

Whenever I glance through photos of my speaking engagements, I reminisce on one of my favorite pictures which depicts two elementary students, a Hispanic boy and an African-American girl standing next to my dad and I near a display table that includes books, pictures and memorabilia from a time in history that readily brings tears and flashbacks from a painful part of my past. A photographer captured the moment and entitled the article, "Remembering the Price They Paid." I thank God for sparing my life to witness that dark day of history where my friends were killed. In life, we all have ups and downs, tragedy and pain, peaks and valleys. Truly, my soul is a witness for my Lord, as I reflect on the blessings of my life and where God has brought me from -- a mighty long way. I am reminded of the saying, "If I can think, I can thank."

Now, come and go with me as I share the blessings of one of many experiences of my life and you will see why I am blessed as I share a witness for my Lord!

In June 1962, my family moved to Birmingham, Alabama. My father, Rev. John Cross, was called to pastor the 16th Street Baptist Church. At the age of 12, I felt excited about our move from Richmond, Virginia to a new city and the possibility of meeting new friends. My mom, Almetia Cross, and my siblings, Alma (10), Michael (4), and Lynn (3), began a new journey as we traveled to a new city that literally presented challenges and eventually changed our lives forever.

After meeting new friends and attending a new school, I was adjusting to life in Birmingham, despite the sudden awareness of the segregated south and demonstrations and exposure to signs in stores over water fountains marked "Colored" and "Whites Only."

On Sunday, September 15, 1963, the youth were excited that this was the first youth day service that was established under my dad's pastorate at 16th Street Baptist Church. Many of the youth had roles on program to usher, play in the orchestra, sing in the choir or participate on program. My role was to sing with the youth choir. Immediately, after Sunday school the Worship Service Hour would start at 11:00a.m. All of the youth classes were in the basement of the church and the adult classes were held upstairs in the main sanctuary. After studying the Sunday school lesson for the day, "A Love That Forgives" and the conclusion of the class, I met my friend outside my class and we planned to go to the bathroom before we prepared to go to the worship service. However, my Sunday School teacher stopped me and gave me a clerical assignment for Sunday school that literally spared my life and kept me from harm's way. I gave my friend my wallet and told her that I would see her after completing my assignment. Approximately 10 or 15 minutes later, while working on my assignment, there was a horrific noise and I remember something hit my head; I later realized it was the light fixture. The building seemed to sway and shake under my feet, I remember everything getting real dark and smelling horrible fumes and hearing the screams and cries of children.

The aftermath of that day seemed gloomy and sad for a long time. I became nervous and developed hands that constantly trembled. I began having nightmares, and I seemed to always hear that horrible noise. Approximately a month after that day, my

98

elementary teacher sent me to another teacher's room. This was the classroom of one of my church members, Mrs. Maxine McNair, who greeted me and had a huge manila envelope for me. When I opened the envelope, I shook and sobbed, when I removed the contents, it was my powder blue wallet that I had given to my friend Addie Mae Collins (14), one of the victims that died in the bombing. The other girls killed were Denise McNair (11), daughter of Chris and Maxine McNair, Carole Robertson (14) and Cynthia Wesley (14).

On Sunday, September 14, 2008, I returned to Birmingham, Alabama and attended the worship service and the celebration for the completion of the renovation project of the 16th Street Baptist Church that is now a National Historic Landmark. U.S. Representative Autor Davis spoke and read a letter from then-Democratic Presidential Candidate, Barack Obama. A new marker outside the church was unveiled depicting the four little girls in silhouette with their arms around each other looking toward the church. This marker commemorates the 45th anniversary of the church bombing.

Yes, my soul will continue to be a "witness for my lord" as I share about the atrocities in the South and share the social changes that evolved. Also, I remember the Sunday school lesson, "A Love that Forgives," the type of Godly love where you are rooted and grounded to love and forgive those who persecute you. This lesson I will continue to witness and keep the memory of my four friends alive.

Barbara Cross, a native of Richmond, Virginia and a graduate of Tuskegee University in Tuskegee, Alabama. Her father was the pastor of the 16th Street Baptist Church in Birmingham, Alabama where on Sunday, September 15, 1963, a bomb exploded that killed the four little girls. Currently, Ms. Cross shares her historical experience with audiences nationwide.

We are Climbing Jacob's Ladder, Soldiers of the Cross
Rudine Freeman

"Because of the Lord's great love we are not consumed, for His compassions never fail." ~ Lamentations 3:22

It is about two in the morning and God suddenly awakens me to pray. I've only been in bed for about an hour and now I'm up again praying. However, the air is crisp and the atmosphere is quiet. Specific instructions are easy to hear. "Pray for Amanda," was my command. When you do not know how to pray the Holy Spirit will intercede and pray through you.

I did not know how to pray or what to pray for my daughter, Amanda. So I yielded to the Holy Spirit and prayed in tongues for Amanda. As a result the voice of God was clear, and with much urgency, spoke, "Amanda is living a sloppy lifestyle. Go and get her."

It had only been two years since Amanda entered Tuskegee University. The thought of going to get her was heartbreaking. After all, Amanda was now in the middle of her new beginning. I did not want her fresh start interrupted. Considering my recent contacts all of the signs were there. My telephone calls were never returned and the excuses from her roommate were ridiculous. The truth could not be avoided. This issue had surfaced and was not going to disappear without being resolved. Amanda definitely was not staying in the dormitory where I left her.

I resorted to leaving a firm message with her roommate. "Tell Amanda that I will be there on Saturday morning to pick her up. She must have all of her belongings packed and ready to go. Tell her that her mother said that she'd better be at the room where I left her. Tell her that if she does not obey, the city of Tuskegee will know who I am because I will turn the place upside down! Do you understand the message?"

A soft, "Yes ma-am," responded.

Every Round Goes Higher and Higher

Traveling from Atlanta to Tuskegee, Alabama was TIME... TIME to pray, TIME to listen.

"Oh Lord if it be possible, let this cup pass from me. Nevertheless, not as I will but thy will be done," was my prayer.
The confrontation was not only with Amanda but also with a group of her friends. They were all waiting outside of her dormitory. There were tears, whispering and conversation between them. Someone finally had the nerve to ask me would I consider letting her stay and finish the semester. I responded with a look that answered.

My truth was from God to get her out of here. The campus was basically quiet and still. The angels had prepared the way. In the midst of the emotions I made the statement, "Let's all help to load this truck as quickly as possible. Thank you very much."

I prayed, "God, help me. I need your strength, your courage. Hold my hands, keep my heart and calm my spirit."
The truck was loaded in less than an hour. Amanda finally looked at me and requested, "Can I go to his house and get my TV.

Instead of slapping her, I simply answered, "NO!" (Remember, I prayed that God would hold my hands). She was reminded that everything had to be at the dormitory.

If You Love Him Why Not Serve Him?

The trip home was quiet. I thought a little about God's providential care. But I thought a lot about me, me, me! My hurt! My pain! My sacrifice! My wasted money and time! My embarrassment! God quickly showed me so much about myself as I lingered in this tunnel of darkness. His power and gentle voice said, "This is not about you. This is about ME and who I AM. Look at her. Stop glancing at her and look at her." The tears started flowing down my face. I saw pain, fear, stress and uncertainty in her eyes.

I prayed, "Lord, let your love and your Word lift us up and carry us out of this like you did for Shadrach, Meschach and Abednego: unscarred. Keep us in your arms of strength and comfort. Thank you for this victory."

Amanda later confided in me that she was living with the campus drug dealer. Her lifestyle was dangerous and detrimental to her and others. Hearing and obeying God had protected as well as saved her life.

Changes, changes and more changes have taken place in the past years. My healing has directly affected Amanda's healings. I sense and see her emotions moving into a positive and healthy vein. First I had to watch myself overcome anger, fear and hurt. This is a daily transformation, and a moment by moment process. I willingly submit to the process. I love Him and I want to serve Him. I am climbing Jacob's ladder.

Become a Solider of The Cross

To God be the glory, honor and praise for the marvelous things he is continuously doing in Amanda's life. Amanda is now a light to many young ladies, helping to transform their lives. I love Amanda, my daughter; Amanda the mother and sister. Thank you for being the God who is more than enough.

God says my people will perish because of a lack of knowledge. This testimony assures you that God can do anything but fail. I welcome you to become one of His children by praying this prayer.

"Father God, I believe that Jesus is your son and that He died on the cross for me and He was resurrected so that I might have eternal life. I repent of my sins and thank you for forgiving me. I release forgiveness for others. I accept Jesus Christ as my Lord and Savior. Thank you, God, for receiving me as your child. I am saved."

Rudine Freeman graduated with honors from Jacksonville Theological Seminary and is founder of Love in Action Agency. She is the mother of three children, a writer, educator and speaker. She is committed to the ministry of intercession. She encourages others and helps them to resolve the issues of life with the practical application of the Word of God.

Abundant Life Realized

"Ain't Gonna Let Nobody Turn Me 'Round"
Rev. Jini Kilgore Cockroft

"Our heart has not turned back, nor have our steps departed from your way..." ~ *Psalm 44:18*

I do not remember singing, "Ain't Gon' Let Nobody Turn me 'Round" in the church when I was growing up. Instead, I encountered the song as a young adult when I worked in the South with the Civil Rights Movement in 1969. Since then, the song has stuck with me. It is a song about determination that I have heard in the back of my mind many times. Some years ago it serenaded me when I was struggling with self-determination - knowing myself and doing those things that were right for me.

Previously, I had seemingly followed a scent that led me to a fork in the road. To the left–"preparation;" and to the right, "activation." Somehow, I got preparation by studying the subjects that complemented my God-given abilities. So, when preparation directed me to add the pursuit of Christian ministry in seminary to my career in writing, all was well. But when I was asked, "What will you do in ministry?" I answered, "Where He leads me, I will follow," which was a pious way of saying, "I don't know." After seminary I went wherever the doors were open. However, while I was on the target board, especially in local church staff ministries, I was not on the bull's eye. Through much prayer, I realized that fulfilling others' expectations of me, no matter how well meaning, was a poor substitute for activating my unique place in ministry.

Today, thankfully in place, I teach religion courses to prospective and practicing ministers at a Bible college, and my craft (writing) at a university. I also preach, and I write and edit religious writings. Now on the bull's eye, I have learned to say, "Yes!" to what God has for me and just as importantly, "No!" to offers outside of that plan because I "ain't gon' let nobody turn me 'round."

Rev. Jini Kilgore Cockroft is a member of Second Baptist Church in Los Angeles, California and she serves as assistant to her husband, Pastor Willie Cockroft in Highway Ministries, an inner-city mission. She is a graduate of Occidental College, UC Berkeley and The American Baptist Seminary of the West and she is enrolled in the Doctor of Ministry degree program at Haggard School of Theology, Azusa Pacific University.

The Miracle Worker
Mary Magdalene Parker

"Hearing this, Jesus said to Jairus, 'Don't be afraid; just believe, and she will be healed.'" ~ Luke 8:50

It was October 1995 when our daughter, Gail Arnette Parker, informed her family that she discovered a lump in her left breast. We weren't prepared for the results of the biopsy because a lump was discovered in my right breast in 1972 and my biopsy revealed only a cyst. The results of her biopsy sent shock waves through our family. Gail had cancer! My faith in God sustained and strengthened me.

Gail had graduated from Temple University in Philadelphia, after completing her freshman and sophomore years at Clark Atlanta University in Atlanta, Georgia. Gail made the Dean's list at both schools. She was a strong, independent black woman. After her graduation in May 1995, she moved from Philadelphia to Clarkston, Georgia (near Stone Mountain) where a job and an apartment were awaiting her arrival. With ambivalence, her father and I gave her our blessings and she began her new life.

Beginning her journey of healing, Gail underwent a mastectomy. We arrived early the morning of her surgery. Our family anxiously awaited her return from recovery. After the surgery, her doctor came and told us that the surgery had gone well. Her doctor knew that I had come down from Philadelphia to be with Gail and she remarked how nice it was for her mother to come to be with her. With vigor, Gail remarked, "And she brought her entourage with her." Oh, did she have a sense of humor in the midst of pain!

After a few weeks of recuperation, Gail was anxious to get back to work. She asked her supervisor if she would bring work home for her to do, and she did. Soon she returned to work. Her next goal was pursuing a Master's degree in African-American Studies. As the Holy Spirit began revealing things to me, I can see that Gail was on a fast track to get things accomplished. She knew the plans that God had for her and she also knew what she needed to accomplish in 29 years.

In 1997, Gail took her nephew Robert IV (Robby) to Disney World in Florida. She flew to Philadelphia to get Robby and they went back to Georgia. I thought they were flying to Florida, but when Mavis (Gail's sister and my daughter) told me she was driving I simply prayed. I've already stated that Gail was a strong, black woman. The trip was a good one for them.

Gail knew the Lord, she accepted Him early in life. She had no fear; she knew that the Lord was her strength (Psalm 27:1). She began traveling and experiencing the world. She and her friends traveled to the Islands several times. Her friends in Philadelphia loved visiting Gail in Atlanta. Her best friend Cheryl had begun plans to move to Atlanta before Gail transitioned.

Gail loved living in Atlanta. Mavis loved visiting her in Atlanta. They had lots of fun together. Gail loved showing her around, and introducing her to the friends that she met at college. She also loved connecting with a friend, Lamont Wells, who was from Philadelphia. They had attended the same church. They loved getting together with their cousin Monica who lived in Stone Mountain. When her brother-law Robert (Bobby) visited Atlanta on business trips he loved visiting with Gail. When she wanted to relax, eat a great meal and engage in stimulating conversation, she would go to her Aunt Betty and Cousin Monica's home. They lived just across the railroad in Stone Mountain.

It was October 1999; we were devastated to learn that Gail's cancer had returned. We encouraged her to move back to Philadelphia with her family. With mixed emotions she agreed. She had just landed a great job, moved into a spacious town house and now her future seemed gloomy. Saying goodbye to Atlanta was an emotionally wrenching experience for her. Giving up her independence would not be easy. She began to make the adjustments. She was pleased that she would now be able to spend more time with her adorable nephews, Robby and Romier.

Soon I discovered that Gail had begun a pen-pal correspondence with an inmate in the Philadelphia area. This shocked me and the questions began to unfold. Gail and Mavis were very close. Therefore, I asked Mavis about the pen-pal relationship. I learned that Gail had gone online seeking to reach out to someone and to be a source of encouragement and inspiration. She got the opportunity to visit with Henry upon her return home. I believe this was a life-changing experience for both of them. She continued to encourage him and he became a source of encouragement for her during her illness. He was as grateful for her support and friendship as expressed in many letters. One of his letters stated that for the first time he had hope that he would return back to society and become a productive citizen. Looking back I can see that she was on a mission to accomplish what she needed to in her short life. (Jeremiah 1:5, "Before I formed you in the womb I knew you.")

Now it was time to begin those chemotherapy treatments. Upon the recommendation of her oncologist in Atlanta, she went to the University of Pennsylvania Hospital to begin her treatments. It was there where God performed a great miracle. I was to learn about it later. October 27, 1999 began as any ordinary day. Mavis had taken a leave from her job. She was to take Gail for her first treatment. I went to work as usual because I had taken a leave earlier to go to Atlanta and accompany her back home. My co-worker asked me if I was going to the hospital for the 2:00 p.m. appointment. I replied, "My daughter is taking her." At that moment, my spirit said to me, "Go and be with them since this is the first treatment of chemotherapy." I gathered my things and left for the hospital. I am thankful for my coworker asking the right question and for the prompting of the Holy Spirit. When I arrived they were in the waiting area and surprised to see me. We went in the doctor's office. After all the tests were performed her nurse Jane took us to the treatment room. Upon getting Gail in bed the nurse began administering the drugs. When the first drop entered into her veins, she began gasping for breath. The nurse gave her the medication for that type of reaction. Her breathing became worse. The nurse immediately unplugged the tube because, at that time, Gail wasn't responding to the medication. Doctors were called; they arrived quickly. They were there in seconds and sounded code blue. At that point, Mavis and I were taken into a waiting area. We were crying. The nurses were trying to console us. I said, "Lord if I ever needed you I need you now." I fell down on my knees, and began to pray His words back to Him. I prayed:

"Lord Jesus, I have read how you healed the sick and performed miracles. Dear Lord, please touch my daughter, Gail, with your healing hand. Please don't take her from us now; she just came back to live with us after six years. I know you are the same God now that you were when you dwelled here on earth. I know that you have the same healing power and can perform miracles just as you did then. Please touch her right now. In Jesus' name I pray."

As they were taking her to the intensive care unit, the doctor said to us she might not make it. By that time I had a calmness that I didn't understand. We all had gathered around her bed, praying. Other family members began to arrive and began praying. She was in a coma. About 10:00 p.m., the doctors rushed everyone out. Immediately they began code blue again. The doctors came from everywhere, they began inserting more tubes. Our pastor, Rev. John

Richardson, arrived and he prayed. Then he asked us to join the other family members and friends in the waiting room. He said, "I want each one of you to pray," and we did. A bit later the doctor came in and reported to us that she was stable. We began thanking and giving God praise - the beginning of the miracle.

Gail remained in a coma for about two weeks before she began making progress. The third week she began improving, opening her eyes. The miracle was continuously unfolding. We saw the substance of what we had hoped for, evidence of what we had not seen earlier. By the beginning of the fourth week she began talking. We stayed at the hospital day and night. The first two weeks my husband and I stayed at night. The staff made us very comfortable. They provided a room next door where my husband slept, and provided a comfortable couch for me in her room. Mavis would come during the day.

Finally her heart was back to normal. She began her cancer treatments again. When the nurse came in and said, "You are the miracle lady that everybody is talking about,"

Gail said to the nurse, "I heard them saying, 'She is dying.'"

I did not fully understand until much later. On her discharge date, the head cardiologist said to me, "When you all were around her bed praying, 'I saw the Lord standing with you.'" I thank him for how God had used His knowledge to treat Gail.

During our first visit back to the cancer center, the nurses gathered around us in disbelief. One nurse said to me, "When you were praying I wanted to pray, but I didn't know what to say."

The nurse, Jane, who was administering the chemotherapy, said to me, "Mrs. Parker, I never believed in miracles, but I do now because your daughter was gone."

Now, I understood why they called her the miracle lady. Hallelujah! Praise God for His miraculous work.

Later, Gail began treatment at Einstein Hospital upon the recommendation of our family doctor. Dr. Cohen treated her with a new drug. She responded well to the drug. Soon she began doing many of the things she was doing before. She did volunteer work at People TV; it was boring. She worked at Society Hill Furniture Store as a secretary; she loved it because she made her own hours. She had the opportunity to be independent again.

Months later, she traveled back to her beloved Atlanta, a trip provided by her cousin/sister Monica. What a wonderful reunion of family and friends. She also traveled to Columbus, Ohio to our family reunion. She enjoyed life again before the Lord sent the sweet chariot to take her home.

Late fall 2001, her health began to deteriorate. After spending weeks in the hospital, she returned home to the comfort of her room. On Saturday evening, December 29, 2001, at 6:00 P.M., Gail stepped on board the chariot in the presence of her sister Mavis and Cousin Monica, but not before I saw her behold His face. Finally, God, the miracle worker gave her eternal healing.

Mary Magdalene Parker is retired from a 30-year banking career at the Federal Reserve Bank in Philadelphia. She received her diploma in Biblical Studies from Beulah Bible Institute in Philadelphia. With much joy and compassion, she ministers to inmates in the Philadelphia Prison weekly.

Sisters by Choice
Leatrice Reed Roberts

"So we, being many, are one body in Christ, and every one member one of another." ~ Romans 12:5

Being an only child, God has always provided me with sincere Christian friends on this journey of life. In elementary school there was a girl that was in my Sunday school class at church and in the same room with me at school, who was always there sharing conversation and "girl talk." Seventy-five years later, we write, send cards (she loves to receive any type card) and serve as a support system for one another.

In junior high school, God again provided the relationship I needed by sending me a Christian friend. I knew this was a trustworthy friend. Candy bars were three for ten cents at a neighborhood grocery store. After I gave her a nickel and she gave me one and a half candy bars rather than just one like most of the students.

High school was no different. In my homeroom, I was assigned to collect money for war saving stamps, which were later redeemed by the owner for saving bonds. That was one of our contributions to the war effort. Collecting the money and preparing the report was time consuming, making it necessary for me to take part of my lunchtime. A girl that I met at a citywide youth church meeting was in my class and offered to help me prepare my report. Her help made it possible for me to eat lunch and talk to a friend at lunchtime.

September 17, 1945 during freshman orientation in college, two girls were looking forlorn and lost, wondering what was to happen next. Joining in conversation, we found we had similar experiences, likes and dislikes. Through the college years we became friends/sisters and shared life's struggles, joys and pains. It should be noted that each of the sisters by choice became acquainted with one another's family members. Friends, sisters by choice, have been on this journey 75+ years sharing the ceremonies of life: marriages, births, deaths, divorces, grandchildren, great grandchildren and family. As Katrina survivors, these sisters have been such a blessing to my family and me.

Although four sisters were cited in this short story, there have been many others who have befriended me and had an influence on my life and I am a better person for knowing them. All of these sisters by choice are now scattered, each in a different state of these United States.

From our lowly beginnings in New Orleans, Louisiana to this present day - no matter the time, distance or circumstances - we sisters by choice are together in prayer and can always reach one another by modern technology. God has His hand on us. God bless us all.

Leatrice Reed Roberts received a B.A. in Education from Dillard University and a Master of Education from Louisiana State University. She has done extensive work in the area of Child Development. She is lifelong best friend of Dr. Regina C. Anderson. She is married to Mr. Edward Roberts with one son Edward Reed Roberts Jr. and grandson Edward Reed Roberts, Jr.

Love What You Do
Terrie Brown

"And whatever you do, whether in word or deed, do it all in the name of the Lord Jesus, giving thanks to God the Father through him." ~ Colossians 3:17

Over the years I discovered and have come to embrace the truth that loving what you do is more important than what you do. While this belief did not become a reality until much later in my life, I thank God for the revelation.

I came to the realization that more often than not, extremely talented and highly intelligent individuals spend the most productive years of their lives working for someone else and performing tasks that in many instances are not fulfilling. A considerable amount of people work 30 and 40 years in positions they don't like for people that don't like them and earn salaries that are not consistent with what they are worth. Ultimately, their efforts contribute to making someone else extremely wealthy. After 25 years in the workforce, I found myself in a similar situation. The primary difference between me and many of my colleagues is that I came to the conclusion that God had a far greater purpose for my life and I decided to pursue it.

I made a conscious decision to leave my "good paying job" and go into business for myself. If I alluded to the fact that this was an easy decision, let me clarify that it was not. In fact, it was one of the most difficult choices I have ever made. As one might expect, my family could not see the logic in my plan. At one point I think they decided that I had lost touch with reality. The one thing that they were well aware of was when I made up my mind; it was virtually impossible to convince me otherwise. I imagine they must have encountered the same emotions they had experienced when I announced I was packing up and moving my family from Oakland, California to Atlanta, Georgia; but by the grace of God, I did it.

The only way I can explain it is that when God puts something on your heart that He desires to come to fruition, it becomes magnified and continues to grow until it is manifested. My thoughts about leaving the job dominated every part of my being. I experienced an ongoing repetition of just about every emotion imaginable. My emotions went from an unbelievable high and feelings of elation to the lowest debts of doubt, fear and confusion. When I think back to this chapter in my life I now realize why the majority of individuals don't pursue their goals and dreams. It's a pretty frightening step to take. My prayer life increased, as did my prayer requests. At various times I would ask myself if this was a logical decision. During other intervals I was totally confident about my plans. Then there were the times when that little adversary that occasionally occupies space in my head caused my faith to waiver and forced me to think about the possibilities of failure. What if my plan didn't work?

What if my income was not adequate to pay my mortgage and other essential expenses? While I was not absolutely sure if the choice was a rational one, the one thing that was completely clear in my mind was that I was totally dissatisfied with the demands of my job and the inequities I not only witnessed but that I also experienced. It was apparent to me that those feelings were not likely to change.

After much vacillating and contemplation I decided to step out on faith. I left my job and started working full time as an independent contractor in the financial services industry. It was quite an adjustment. I love the freedom and flexibility that it offers. I love helping people to learn about money and become better stewards over their finances. I can honestly say that I have tremendously impacted numerous lives in significant ways. A recent situation involved a client who died 30 days after we placed an income protection life insurance program on her life. Her husband who killed himself and almost fatally wounded their 2-year-old had killed her. It was one of the most tragic scenarios I have ever experienced. Several months after her claim was processed, I delivered to her mother and two other children a check for $350,000. The mother was so grateful that I was able to impact their family that she entrusted me to invest the majority of the money so that the children would have some degree of financial security.

Needless to say, becoming an entrepreneur comes with its own unique set of circumstances. One of the first lessons that I learned was that freedom wasn't free. If I wanted to eat, I was going to have to work just as hard for myself as I had worked for others. Adjusting to the fact that I was now my own boss took some time. I really had to work at establishing a schedule and adhering to it. It was so easy to lose focus, waste time, run errands for other people and get off task. After all, I had no one to report to except myself.

Part of my obsession to gain independence in the business world was due, in large part, to my entrepreneurial-minded family. My mom was a licensed barber for almost 40 years. I recall spending hours helping her prepare for her state exam. The entire family was ecstatic when she passed her test. She absolutely loved working in this field and was quite skilled at her craft. Her clients loved and respected her and she in turn was forever grateful for their ongoing support. I spent a considerable amount of time at the shop running errands and cleaning up in the evenings and on the weekends. I'm confident that some of her entrepreneurial drive had an impact on my spirit. While I was not fully cognizant of it then, when I look back she was in a really great position. She was one of the first African American female barbers in the city of Oakland. As an independent agent she was in a position to make all the decisions affecting her business. She also made a good living and had the freedom and flexibility to manage her time and activities in the manner that she chose.

In addition to my mom, I also have a brother and sister who, for many years, have had their own businesses. Both did quite well in real estate investing and were rather passionate about it. They influenced me to invest in real estate, which I absolutely love. It must be in our genes. My sister also owned a vintage clothing shop where she sold some of the finest apparel from the 30's and 40's. It was an incredible place where I spent hours trying on some of the most divine attire I had ever seen, not to mention all the money I spent.

My decision to leave the workforce was also influenced by some of the gross injustices that I encountered and witnessed throughout the years. I've always been a very dedicated, conscientious team player who pulled her own weight and the weight of certain teammates who refused to do their jobs. Unfortunately, being a hard worker was not the essential characteristic for recognition or advancement. Various unwritten criteria appeared to exist. For example, vacancy announcements were posted for positions with clear qualification requirements. In a number of instances the justification provided for selecting certain individuals had no bearing on the original criteria. In essence the selections were made based on arbitrary criteria that had nothing to do with the evaluation guidelines we expected.

I recall one appraisal period in particular; every non-minority in the office received a rather generous bonus for outstanding performance. This was a blatant injustice because everyone knew who the slackers were and even they received large bonuses if they were of the right persuasion. I found this situation so appalling that I expressed my concerns to management. The question I posed to my boss was, "Can you honestly conclude that not one non-white staff member met or exceeded your expectations during the entire year?" She insisted that whites were not the only employees to get bonuses. I took it upon myself to go through the office roster with her and identify each person who received a bonus, which supported my allegation. As one might expect, she was oblivious to my concerns and attempted to make light of the situation. She continued to deny that any inappropriate action had taken place on her part in spite of evidence to the contrary. This conversation was one of the most defining moments in my career. I found her response to my concerns quite demeaning. After this discussion I began to look at my options and made a decision to seek employment elsewhere. I came to the conclusion that certain practices were so deeply imbedded in the system and part of the overall office culture that they were not likely to change anytime soon.

I'm convinced that the ultimate and overwhelming decision to walk away from a "secure" and "comfortable" job that deposited a paycheck in my bank account every two weeks was that God planted inside me seeds of greatness. I understand that when you plant good seeds in good soil, you reap a bountiful harvest. He also convinced me that my life has no limits or boundaries except the ones that I place on it. He assures me that because of the power and authority He has bestowed upon my life that there is nothing I cannot accomplish if I trust Him and consult Him every step of the way. He reminds me that I am "more than a conqueror." Because I believe and trust in Him, I was able to take this leap of faith. He truly is my comforter and I am so grateful and honored to be a part of His master plan.

Terrie Brown, a native of Oakland, California, for 14 years, has been a personal financial analyst who empowers families with basic financial principles. She conducts many seminars throughout her community and the United States. She graduated from Cal State Hayward in Hayward, California. Ms. Brown attends New Birth Missionary Baptist Church in Lithonia, Georgia. She serves as a board member of Sisters On The Journey, Inc. Her current place of residence is Stone Mountain, Georgia and she is the mother of two sons, Brian and Jason.

Living My Dreams Wide Awake
Cheryl Ward

"Delight yourself in the LORD and he will give you the desires of your heart." ~ Psalm 37:4

I'll never forget the day I heard my friend, Tiffini, make the declaration, "I'm living my dreams wide awake." It resonated in my spirit and I began expressing my gratitude to the Lord because that is exactly what I am doing too. It took a long time and lots of mixed up priorities to understand that the people I love and the ones who love me are the most important things in my life. I spent many years chasing accomplishments and pseudo-success, believing that it was the bane of my fulfillment. Education and career pursuits were totally based on my perception of "the crowd's" expectations. I soon came to accept that I did not *need* another degree and wasn't really doing my "passion" work.

This epiphany inspired me to list all of the things that I said I would do "one day" and made it the task of the current day. My new pursuits were solely based on my heart's desire. For years, I said I would work with teens on a full-time basis, and spend my time just writing and preaching if I had enough money. Once I started pursuing the passion instead of the money, the windows of Heaven opened up for me. A local school district and community college recruited me as a Project Director for a program assisting high school students in passing the California. High School Exit Exam. Upon completion of the contract I was blessed to work from home writing more books and preaching every Sunday. I also have more time and energy to spend with those in my intimate circle; something I had so often taken for granted.

There are days when I find myself smiling at the mere thought that "someday" is today! We, as women, spend our lives ensuring that our spouses reach their goals and our children pursue their dreams, while simultaneously placing our own on the back burner. Perhaps it is a subconscious belief that we do not deserve what we want or even a conscious belief that we cannot have it. It is this same belief system that must be replaced with faith, prayer and daily affirmations or we will find ourselves in a constant game of tug-of-war with self-sabotage once we receive our heart's desires.

The Ten Commandments teach us to "love our neighbors as we love ourselves." It is virtually impossible to authentically share love with anyone else if we do not render it to ourselves first. Self-care cannot be equated with selfishness or we will never come to know what Jesus meant when he said, "The thief comes to steal, kill and destroy, but I came that you would have life and that more abundantly." I am so grateful that the day came when I stopped day dreaming" and grabbed hold of the words of R&B sensation Jill Scott and started "Living' My Life Like it's Golden."

Rev. Cheryl Denise Ward is a pastor, author, and educator who resides in Oakland, California. She is currently completing a Doctor of Philosophy degree in Human Services Administration at Walden University in Baltimore, Maryland.

Look Into The Mirror and Talk to Yourself
Dr. Regina C. Anderson

"Now we see but a poor reflection as in a mirror; then we shall see face to face. Now I know in part; then I shall know fully, even as I am fully known." ~ 1 Corinthians 13:12

As a child, if I disobeyed, used poor judgment, or did something considered to be wrong, my parents would often send me to the bathroom with the firm direction: "Look into the mirror and talk to yourself." "How stupid!" I would say to myself. "What a senseless punishment." In fact, it was fun, I thought.

The first five or ten minutes seemed senseless fun but I played the game of being obedient to my parents. I would look into the mirror and make funny faces, giggle and do silly things. After about an hour, I began to settle down. Funny faces in the mirror were no longer fun. My thoughts began to shift, reverse and question. A little bit at a time, I began to think about what I had done but still thought this to be a senseless and useless punishment. I didn't hurt in my body, but my thoughts began to run rampage and give me pain. Looking in the mirror began as nonsense but I must admit I began to think more seriously about the "foolish punishment." Was it really foolish? Could I have done things differently, behaved differently? Some of my thoughts were piercing, even painful and shameful. Why did you do this or that – painful to be sure, as my conscience began to speak louder and louder.

As an adult, I still sometimes "play" that game; not in the bathroom but in the car while driving to the store or any place, but it is truly no longer play or a game. Talking to yourself – LOOKING IN THE MIRROR – can be revealing and self searching. It can take you behind the closed doors that no one is privileged to open. It often reflects the events of past years. It may require you to ask for pardon or forgiveness. It may reveal the painful truth that you must make a change or that there is no one to blame for your circumstances but you. Looking in the mirror can be very helpful to those who want to search the soul.

Why not take a look? Look in the mirror and talk to yourself!

Dr. Regina C. Anderson is a retired educator, Christian Educator, ordained minister and founder of Sisters On The Journey. She has her Master's of Education from San Francisco State University; Master's of Divinity in Christian Education from American Baptist Seminary of the West and Doctorate of Ministry from United Theological Seminary. She has one daughter and two grandchildren.

We'll Understand It Better By and By
Bennie Little

"But He said to me, "My grace is sufficient for you, For My power is made perfect in weakness." ~ II Corinthians 12:9

Usually when someone says they want to have a heart to heart conversation it means something serious needs to be discussed. Well, the same applies here. I want to talk to your heart about mine.

I moved to Atlanta from California in January 2000 with the expectation that a new beginning would be a good thing. I felt pretty good about most things and aside from some previous health problems, I felt good physically. For the most part I had been very health conscious: eating right, exercising and drinking plenty of water. But due to the preparation for the move, the move itself and getting settled, I had let some things fall by the wayside.

After being in Atlanta about three months, I started a new job so I began the task of getting back in shape and losing some of the pounds that had showed up; only in certain places, I might add. I noticed that when my daughter and I started our walking regime I would experience a shortness of breath very quickly. Since it had been a while since I'd walked, I figured I was just out of shape so I pushed myself onward and upward. My job was an hour commute away and proved to be very tiring as well. But I decided it was just an adjustment period and would pass.

Soon I began to notice other unusual things happening like swollen ankles and discomfort around my mid-section. By this time I was also beginning to *feel* bad overall most of the time. I was bloated and had no energy. I felt just plain lousy. Next I developed a cough and what felt like congestion in my chest. I thought I'd developed just a bad cold or maybe bronchitis. Then something very frightening started happening; at night when I would lie down I could not breathe in any position. I would literally begin to suffocate. We tend to take breathing for granted, but when you can't-------that's very scary. After a couple of days I became exhausted due to a lack of sleep.

I knew then it was time to see a doctor and after getting a referral from a co-worker I visited one the next day. I explained the most recent symptoms and like we have a tendency to do, gave my layperson's diagnosis. She took my blood pressure and temperature which were both normal. Then she began to listen to my chest. There she lingered for a very long time; asking me to sit, lie and breathe in and out. After what seemed like an eternity she asked if I had ever had a heart murmur. I had not. "Well," she said, "you do now. In fact it is whistling at me. I suspect that you also have fluid on your lungs, but no bronchitis." She ordered a chest x-ray which confirmed the fluid on my lungs which then caused the cough and inability to breathe while lying down. She then said that since my blood pressure was normal and I looked ok, she would let me go home but I had to return the following morning for an eco-cardiogram to try to determine what was happening with my heart. She gave me a prescription for a water pill in order to immediately reduce the fluid buildup.

After getting up the next morning I experienced pain in my right arm and numbness in my fingers. I returned to Piedmont Hospital for my test and shared my experience of pain and numbness with the tech. She suggested that I go back and tell the doctor. I spoke with the nurse and she asked me to have a seat while she spoke with the doctor. In a very short time she returned with a wheel chair and informed me that I was headed for the emergency room.

125

Once there, two nurses began working on me, hooking me up to various machines, drawing blood, etc. A doctor finally came in and told me they suspected I may have had a heart attack. They gave me a large dosage of Lasix to get rid of the fluid. Needless to say, I spent a large amount of time in the bathroom from that point on.

I was kept four hours in the emergency room awaiting test results. As I think back, I was not panic-stricken or worried. Was it because I was no stranger to hospitals or was it due to the peace of God that surpasses all human understanding? I now know it was the latter. Finally, a cardiologist came in with the news. While I had not had a heart attack, my heart had been damaged and was enlarged. He went on to explain the degree of damage. Thus began my heart to heart and my education in Life-Changing Illnesses 101.

I was told that when the heart beats most efficiently, it is given a rating of 65. My heart was rated at 20. In addition, my left valve was leaking which accounted for the fluid on my lungs. They had not determined what had caused the damage. He went on to explain that they would begin a regime of medications to hopefully prevent any further damage. You see, according to medical science, the heart muscle does not regenerate. Once it is damaged, it can only get worse or stay the same. I later found out that one of the medications was a blood thinner. …a pill? I think not but rather, two shots a day in my stomach. I was admitted and another test called a cardiac-catheterization was scheduled for Monday. It was Good Friday.

I was initially diagnosed with congestive heart failure. Once it was determined that my arteries were clear the diagnosis was downgraded to cardio-myopathy. My whole life changed in a matter of weeks. During my stay in the hospital I was reeducated on every aspect of my life: diet, exercise, all day-to-day physical, mental and emotional activity. Every effort had to be made to guard my heart from any exertion. Practically everything one does affects your heart. Sudden changes in body temperature, diet, fluid and sodium intake, emotions, the amount of rest you get and certain over the counter medications.

I started to question God as to why He had let me come way down to Atlanta and as soon as I got a job and started to get settled, to become sick again. I had previously had four major surgeries and recovered from them all with no long-range effects. For this I am thankful. However, this time it was different, even mysterious. Doctors still don't know what caused the damage. Therefore, that good old culprit, the virus, was blamed for attacking my heart. Thus, I began a new journey with the Lord; a little uncertain and sometimes a little scary, but with a renewed trust.

"Trials dark on every hand, and we cannot understand all the ways that God could lead us to that blessed promised land, but He guides us with His eye, and we'll follow till we die, for we'll understand it better by and by."

Some would ask, "What about all the hard work to stay physically fit and eating properly; what's the point if something like this can still happen?" Well, first and foremost God is still in control and has the last word. Secondly, **an ounce of prevention is still worth a pound of cure.** Had my heart not been so strong from all the exercise, it probably would not have been able to withstand the attack. I am now aware of and can share yet another aspect of a woman's health. Heart disease is the #1 killer of women, not breast cancer.

The symptoms of a heart attack are different for a woman than a man, a fact some doctors don't even know or choose to ignore. Therefore, we must be our own advocates. Educate yourself and please know there is always room for improvement. Exercise; watch your fat, sugar and salt intake. We tend to get caught up on our fat intake and forget about sugar and salt. Get the proper rest and laugh as often as you can. Laughter is music to the soul and an excellent stress buster. Also, high blood pressure can destroy your kidneys! NEWS FLASH!

I left the hospital with six medications. I was still a little tired, but thankful. I did not lose my job, but returned a week later. I eventually regained my stamina and can now walk five miles. I am now taking just two medications and have never experienced side effects from any of them. I am and will be on a low-salt diet for life. I lost 16 pounds and the last time I had a cardio test, my heart was rated at 50 (up from 20). So much for medical science, limited at best.

Fast forward to 2007...After seven years my heart has tested better than ever before and it is down to normal size. I've lost 22 pounds and counting, my blood pressure and cholesterol are lower than ever, and I take medication only when I feel like it, just to humor my doctor since he thinks the medications are responsible for my complete recovery. "By and by, when the morning comes;. All the saints of God are gathered home; we'll tell the story how we've overcome for we'll understand it better by and by."

There is still only one Master Physician – To God be the glory!!

Bennie Little grew up in the Oakland/San Francisco Bay Area of California, but her roots are deeply embedded in Hattiesburg, Mississippi, where she was born. She presently resides in the greater Atlanta area and is the proud mother of one daughter and two grandchildren, a 3-year-old and a 14-month old. Bennie is looking forward to the next phase of her life – retirement; confident that it will hold even greater experiences as she allows God to lead her.

The Chaperone: His Eye Is On The Sparrow
Charlotte Harrell

...He leads me beside quite waters, He restores my soul. He guides me in paths of righteousness for His Name's sake.
 Psalm 23:2b

I am called to share my intimate relationship with God. God, you are my Chaperone! When I examine the word, Chaperone, I extract the French root word meaning "head covering: or broadly defined; one delegated to ensure proper behavior.

We often picture a Chaperone as one who escorts or is present at parties/school dances to assure appropriate behavior. A Chaperone is one who knows the complete itinerary of the event; stays a distance to allow the participants to have their experiences and is watchful that the persons they are chaperoning display appropriate behavior."

The thread, that has been consistent throughout my journey, is God is my Chaperone. God, in His infinite wisdom is my heavenly Chaperone. While on this earthly journey, He has blessed me with earthly Chaperones.

My life's journey has taken me through many unusual, unpredictable, non-traditional experiences. I was nurtured and validated in my home, my church family and my neighborhood elementary and middle school. I was satisfied to follow in the neighborhood high school path of my older brothers and sisters. My earthly Chaperone, my mom, consulted with my heavenly Chaperone, God, and new plans were put into place.

After many School Board meetings, a group of students were identified to institute the Open Enrollment Program: an attempt to integrate the new high school. I was shocked to learn that I was one of the identified students. I certainly had not volunteered for the "experiment." We were uprooted from our familiar neighborhood school environment to attend a high school that seemed way, way, way across town. At the time, it seemed like cruel and unusual punishment; having to get up really early; take two and sometime three buses; many times walking up the hill when the bus couldn't make it; using my family's money to pay for bus fare; not feeling a sense of belonging, but rather a sense of having to prove that I belonged. Why did my heavenly Chaperone want me to have this experience? Why did my earthly Chaperone concur, make the financial sacrifices and give me the emotional support to complete this three year journey?

I wanted an immediate revelation and I just wasn't satisfied with the response that the answers would come "by and by". Remember, I was a teen and my faith was just being cultivated. Later, I learned that this was just the initiation for the many experiences to come. I had the assurance that my heavenly Chaperone, who knows the complete itinerary, would be with me and allow me to travel the path that He purposed for me and to monitor my behavior. His expectation in all of my experiences: Can you give your heavenly Chaperone the glory?

I was blessed to complete graduate school. I was granted favor and my two year program was paid in full with scholarships and grants. God was my Chaperone! I returned home, with plans to work and give back to my family who had made so many sacrifices. I especially had plans for my mother; to travel, shop, dine out and just hang out. One year after I returned home, my mom died. I was totally devastated and could not believe that my earthly Chaperone was gone. Even though, she had now joined my heavenly Chaperone, I was not happy. I could only remind my heavenly Chaperone that I was only twenty-four years old and it wasn't fair. How could I trust God? Now, He really had to prove the words of the song," His eye is on the sparrow and I know He watches me." It took me a while to internalize the stanza, "I sing because I'm happy." I was not" feeling" God as my Chaperone. Both Chaperones staged a tag team effort and my thoughts were bombarded with the reminders from my earthly chaperone…remember the scriptures you were taught. "…trust in the Lord and lean not to your understanding…"; "…I have never seen the righteous forsaken or his seed begging bread…": "…I will lift my eyes to the hills from whence cometh my help…"; "…the Lord is my shepherd." Okay, I got the message; my heavenly Chaperone is with me; He knows the complete itinerary and He wants me to show appropriate behavior. So, stop complaining and start praising!

My heavenly Chaperone knew that I needed another earthly Chaperone to mentor and model the appropriate behavior for Christian women. I was invited to participate in a Christian Education workshop at Allen Temple Baptist Church and **there she was**. I kept asking," Who is this lady that has you doing lesson plans for workshops; staying at church until 11pm assembling "packets/ binders"; decorating the Fellowship Hall; serving the Regional Delegates; then washing over 100 place settings of dishes?" At first, they did not tell me her name. The harmonious answer was, "…and don't worry about staying late or getting here early; she will feed you." I later learned that she answered to many names and I could decide which earthly Chaperone title fit me. She was called Mrs. Lady, Mrs. Anderson, Mrs. Regina, and later, Reverend Anderson and Dr. Anderson. Later, along with some of the young women she mentored (a trusted counselor or guide, a tutor/coach), we created our own names: Reverend Mother; What Regina Wanteth, She Geteth: and finally Nanan, the Creole word for God-Mother.

I embraced my new earthly Chaperone and felt a sense of belonging by calling her Nanan. I am "awestruck" at how God has allowed our paths to cross and intertwined our lives in some of the most unusual, unpredictable and non-traditional ways. To God be the glory.

I am thankful to my heavenly Chaperone for the assurance that He has the complete itinerary; He allows me to have the experiences that are part of my divine purpose and He guides my behavior so that He gets the glory in all that I experience.

"I sing because I'm happy. I sing because I'm free. His eye is on the sparrow and I know He watches me."

Charlotte Harrell is an elementary school teacher in Oakland, California. She is committed to teaching the "whole child." Her motto "...the destiny of my life is in His hands, where he leadth, I will follow."

Praise God FromWhom All Blessings Flow

My Spiritual Journey
Pamella J. Williams, Ph.D.

"Show me your way, O Lord, teach me your paths; guide me in your truth for you are God my Savior, and my hope is in you all day long." ~ Psalm 25:4-5

Paul, in his letter to the Corinthian Church, writes, "I have planted, Apollos watered; but God gave the increase" (I Corinthians 3:6) . . . and so my story begins. How I came to accept Christ as my Lord and Savior resembles, I guess, a hooked fish being reeled into shore. Many years have gone by and as I reflect on these years and look forward to those years remaining, I realized that I have been on a spiritual journey for all of my life.

As a child, I attended church with my friends because it was more of a social rather than a spiritual thing to do. I always enjoyed the "pomp and circumstance" and the beauty of the church I attended. I memorized the liturgies and prayers and was basically a "Sunday only" attendee participating in church activities only as they addressed my social circle of friends. I most certainly did not consider myself to be a sinner. And, as for salvation . . . never heard of such a thing! But one thing I did know – I hadn't killed anyone or done anything I considered to be really wrong. I loved my parents, my church, America and apple pie. How much better could I be?

Attending church in the 1960s was a time of social change – from the pulpit. I would hear stories of the civil rights movement, women were entering the ministry for the first time and changes were being made to our church denomination's standard order of worship. Services addressed cultural and civil issues as opposed to spiritual issues. I continued, as in my youth to be a Sunday only attendee; I would hear the message and leave.

As I grew into adulthood, married and started a family, there was a growing sense of discontent in my sense of religion, my Christianity, as I knew it. There was something missing. Oh well . . . I decided to not be too concerned about the matter. I was indeed, having the time of my life – a wonderful husband and two great children. I was actively involved in a wide range of social and civic activities. But still there was a little dark cloud hanging over me that simply could not be identified. About this time my family and I moved to a town where my husband's former roommate now lived with his wife. Jerry's former roommate had been an agnostic and now he and his wife were telling of what Christ had done for them; and they continually referred to Christ as their Lord and Savior. I must admit that I had no idea what they were talking about.

The Seed Was Planted.

The wife of this couple was a firm believer in the power of prayer and spoke incessantly of "faith." On and on she would share her story peppered with words such as "faith," "mercy and grace," etc. Was I listening? Yes I was!! With some annoyance, I will admit, but continuing to hear what she had to say.

One day my young son and I happened upon a gumball machine. I included this in my story because the incident is one I will never forget. Laurence said, "Mommy, I would like to have a green one, please," in yes, simple childlike faith. And, he put his penny in the machine and out came, yes, you've guessed it – the green gumball!! By chance? Perhaps, but I didn't think so. I didn't quite understand the extreme joy and excitement I felt, but nevertheless it was there. I thought maybe there is something to what my new friends were talking about.

Sitting Sunday after Sunday in church, I began to identify the problem I was having. There was no real sense of true Bible teaching or the interpretation of scriptures. The message of salvation was there in the prayers and liturgies, but I saw that message only after I attended a church that was truly Bible based and then I came to understand these prayers that I had previously learned in rote memorization. Sermon after sermon addressed the civil and social issues of the times and the helping of others in need – but nothing really significant was learned or absorbed about the Word of God.

Then came another move, this time to Evanston, Illinois and would you believe it – this time we met a former high school friend of my husband's and his wife. And yes, they too had become born-again Christians! They would visit us night after night and offer God's plan of salvation over and over, again and again.

The Seed Was Watered.

One day, my husband and I, in the quietness of our living room, acknowledged ourselves to be sinners and asked Jesus Christ to come into our lives. We quietly asked for forgiveness and accepted Christ as our Lord and Savior. There were no shooting stars or roaring winds of burning bushes. It seemed too easy, too simple. One day, I read John 1: 12, "But as many as received Him, to them gave He the power to become the sons of God, even to them that believe in His name." I knew, beyond any doubt, that I was a child of God. It wasn't by my good deeds or works that I became His child but because I believed.

Over the years, I have had my ups and downs in life and I have to cling desperately to my faith in a just and righteous God when circumstances and events seemed to appear as if I served an absent and much uninvolved God. But there has always been a fellow sojourner with a prayer, a pat on the back and an "I understand what you're going through" that has gotten me back on track. I have also known tremendous joys and highlights in my Christian walk, truly reveling in the joy of the Lord! Along the journey, I have grown and developed and matured in my life in Christ. I eagerly look forward to see what the Lord will bring my way knowing that God, in His mercy, will provide the way to accomplish His purpose for my life.

God Gave the Increase.

In this "topsy turvy" world in which we live, I sometimes wonder how anyone can live without hope in the just and righteous God who created the universe and all things within it. It gives me peace to know that I am just passing through this life and that, one day, I will be with the Lord for all eternity. I am truly blessed, at peace and so very thankful for my life in Christ.

"But they that wait upon the Lord shall renew their strength
they shall mount up with wing as eagles;
they shall run and not be weary; and
they shall walk, and not faint."
Isaiah 40: 31

Pamella J. Williams, Ph.D. retired in 2003. She has served on the Board of Directors for the North Shore Country Day School and its Women's Board in Winnetka; board member of the Mental Health Agency of Evanston, Illinois; and as an elder of First Presbyterian Church of Evanston, Illinois. She was a director of the Evanston Historical Society and President of the Lynda Martha Dance Troupe in Evanston, Illinois.

Take My Hand, Precious Lord
Sheila A. Coley

"Therefore, since we are surrounded by so great a cloud of witnesses, let us also lay aside every weight and the sin that clings so closely, and let us run with perseverance the race that is set before us, looking to Jesus, the pioneer and perfecter of our faith..." ~ Hebrews 12:1-2

How does the same sky that reveals the brilliant brightness of a sunshiny day and gives warmth to encourage countless outdoor activities become a sky that is dark and seemingly void of life except the bolts of lightning and clashing sounds of thunder that sends everyone scurrying indoors? I exist in this place of time looking in the mirror at myself wondering what happened to the life that I had filled with brilliant sunshine and fulfilling activities.

Life has become encumbered with the darkness of confusion, indecisiveness, hints of anxiety and depression that feel like lighting and thunder shattering my hopes and dreams. Marriage and financial challenges have been compounded with the loss of my daddy to cancer, the concern for my mom and the desire to parent God's way. With far more questions than answers, I am learning to live at peace with the questions. The same mirror that shows me where I can go also shows me where I have been; and that "stuff" is a real indicator that God has never left me nor forsaken me.

As I continue my journey through the green pastures of paradise and the tumultuous terrains of my life, I am reminded by my friend, the late Mother Fannie Hatchett, " Every day will not be sunshine or rain." With confident expectation of the storm passing, I lift my spirit to say:

Precious Lord, take my hand. Lead me on

Let me stand. I'm tired, I am weak, I am worn.

Through the storm, through the night

Lead me on to the light.

Take my hand, precious Lord, lead me home.

When my way grows dear, Precious Lord, linger near.

When my light is almost gone.

Hear my cry, hear my call, Hold my hand lest I fall.

Take my hand, precious Lord, lead me home.

Sheila A. Coley is a powerful motivational speaker in the area of financial and leadership topics with the spiritual gifts of teaching and administration. She earned a Communications degree from Howard University. She is a member of Greenforest Community Baptist Church in Decatur, Georgia. She is a wife and mother of two children.

Nobody Knows The Trouble I've Seen
Jill Jones

"For your maker is your Husband- the Lord Almighty is His name. The Holy One of Israel is your Redeemer; He is called the God of all the earth." ~ Isaiah 54:5

My life looked good...it was supposed to. It was supposed to look like I was running the household. It was designed like that; I started covering up right away. Nobody knows the trouble I've seen. You would never know that it was not as good as it appeared.

I was in church activities alone, PTA alone, community activities alone. I was told to "Tell them I have something more important to do." Participation usually came as the result of an argument. No one knew what I was REALLY going through.

I never saw my parents fight so I did not know what to do. The God in me told me early on (year two of the marriage) to argue back. "Don't let your children think that it is okay for someone to yell at you and you say nothing." So I learned how to argue or to just be quiet. Later I learned not to fight about everything. **Nobody knows the trouble I've seen.**

I became the "cover up queen." I loved him and was determined to make this marriage work, at whatever cost. We had children right away. He was a good father. That's good - right?

Glory Hallelujah!

Sometimes I'm up. I was blessed to be able to become a fulltime mom. I was never an equal partner in the marriage. I did not recognize the control until I stopped working...had to deal with it. **Sometimes I'm down,** We went into business. Life was good. Nice trips, nice neighborhood, nice cars. It looked real good. Financial issues ensued, but everybody has those - right? It's how you handle them. How could it be that bad, I am a saver not a spender. **Although you see me going along, I have trials here below. Yes, Lord!** God kept me. **Nobody knows but Jesus.** He knew everything. I was on my knees throughout the marriage, thanking God for his grace and mercy. I praise Him. **Glory Hallelujah.**

Life changed. I had to take over the business so he could go back to school. I did not know it, but business was going down. I worked 7 days a week to turn it around and keep the household going. It was the only source of family income, and now it is all on me! **Sometimes I'm almost to the ground.** I am not a business woman! I am an educator. I don't know what to do! I need help. I had to figure it out on my own. School was too time consuming. Cover up. Little by little I got the business back on its feet. Like the bumble bee, I did not know I wasn't supposed to succeed. It has been six years and years the business is thriving and I have watched myself grow into a business woman - some say successful.

After twenty one years, he tells me that I don't compromise or listen and we should probably take care of this. What a shocker! What!??? At first I ignored this, what do I do with this information? Surely he doesn't mean what I think he means.

Nobody knows the trouble I've seen, nobody but Jesus! If you get there before I do, tell all my friends I'm coming to. I left. I have peace of mind. The Lord will continue to lead me. **Glory Hallelujah.**

Jill Jones is a native of Nashville, Tennessee. She graduated from Fisk University with a B.A. in English Literature and a M.Ed. from University of Virginia in Counseling in Higher Education. She owns and operates Reading Phonics Math & More, the tutoring center in Stone Mountain, Georgia since 2002. She is the mother of two daughters.

Tramping....Tramping....
Trying to Make Heaven My Home
Catherine Cowling

"Finally, brethren, what ever things are true, whatever things are honest; whatever things are just, think on these things." ~ Philippians 4:8

My journey began in the city of my birth, New Orleans, Louisiana. My father was from Kingston, Jamaica; my mother was a New Orleans native. My first experience with trauma was at a very young age when, during the middle of the night, the authorities came and forcibly took my father out of my mother's bed and deported him back to Jamaica. What pain! Can you imagine how horrible it was for a little girl to helplessly watch strangers, the police, take her father away without knowing where? I didn't see him again until I was 16 when he was allowed to join the United States Maritime Convoy Fleet during World War II.

During all those years my mother struggled as a single parent to rear my brother and me. It was her Christian upbringing, devotion to God, and placing us in a positive environment that would nurture our spiritual and developmental growth. We were church children; Sunday school, Baptist Training Union, Bible Study, and all of our friends were church friends. The church provided our social life and gave me scholarships to go to school to further my education. My church was always a solid rock on which I could stand. It was through the church that all the gifts I was blessed with were discovered and recognized. The church's encouragement was responsible for the journey I sojourned. At an early age I was exposed to a minister who worked diligently with the children emphasizing Christian character and the value of spiritual guidance. The expectation was that we acquire a large vocabulary, become astute in critical and independent thinking, and analyzers of vocal and written expression. This training prepared me for leadership in my spiritual and secular endeavors.

Consequently, I have served as Sunday school superintendent, director of Vacation Bible School, church historian, president of many church organizations and keynote and principal speaker for church, civic and local and national organizations. In Oakland, I served as Sunday school teacher, advisor to Guild Girls and director of an after school study center funded by the Ford Foundation. Currently, I serve as leadership development chairperson of the Lillian Perry Circle of my church.

Vocationally I was in the field of Public School Education, commencing as a teacher and climaxing as an administrator. In addition, I served as Adjunct Professor at San Francisco State University and Graduate Student Field Supervisor at California State University at Hayward.

All of my higher education was afforded through scholarships. I was the recipient of a four- year scholarship from my church in New Orleans, culminating in the Bachelor of Arts degree bestowed by Dillard University at New Orleans. A graduate scholarship in school administration was given to me by Xavier University of New Orleans and the San Francisco Foundation Graduate Fellow, culminating in a Master's degree in Special Education.

My mother constantly reminded me that while life is a journey filled with trials and tribulations, the sun always finds a way to creep through. That is my motto which has undergirded my life. It has governed my directions and expectations of the challenges confronting me. It is encouraging to know that God has always been my source and strength I am still on the journey that was embedded in my life as a small child. Many Christian women have been my role models. Consequently, I too have strived to walk upright.

As an African American Christian woman, we must be godly in our walk before the generation that is following so that they can see the spirit of Jesus within us.

Catherine Cowling is a native of New Orleans, Louisiana and resides in Oakland, California. She is a graduate of Dillard University and completed work for a Master's of Arts in School Administration at Xavier University in New Orleans, Louisiana. She also holds a Master's degree in Special Education from San Francisco State University. She is a retired administrator from Oakland Unified School District and the mother of one son.

Smiling Through the Storms
Dr. Dovie Wesley Gray

"God is our refuge and strength, an ever present help in trouble."
~ Psalm 46:1

I listened quietly by the bedroom door as my parents were trying to make a big decision: whether to give me $75 or $100 for my journey to Atlanta. This was going to be a major sacrifice for my parents. I was the youngest of 11 children, and that money could have bought plenty of groceries for our family. I was pacing the floor while my parents were in the other room deciding my fate. It was an exciting, scary time! I had just graduated from college, and I was headed to "Hotlanta." It was January 1974. Maynard Jackson had just been elected Atlanta's first black mayor, and I had been accepted into Atlanta University's graduate school. There were two major problems. I was going to have very little money - at this point, none - and I had no place to live. However, my master plan was to find a room at the local YWCA and go to the financial aid office to secure a loan to begin my program. My dream was to receive my Master's degree in Guidance and Counseling and become a school counselor. I had completed college in three and a half years. I was going to become a teacher while I worked on my graduate courses. It sounded so simple.

My parents finally came out of the bedroom, giving me the exciting news that I would be receiving $100. I smiled. With my cash and my bus ticket, I was ready to begin my journey. For you non-bus-riders, I need to explain what riding the bus meant. Greyhound was considered first class; it stopped only at major cities like Little Rock, Memphis, Nashville and Birmingham. On the other hand, Trailways, the bus that I took, stopped in every tiny town from Springfield, Arkansas to Atlanta, Georgia – Conway, Menifee, Pine Bluff, Plumerville, Russellville and the list goes on. That was okay with me. I was smiling as I boarded the bus, waving goodbye to my parents and saying hello to an uncertain future. While riding through those tiny towns, I had opportunities to reflect over my life. As I was staring out at the countryside, looking at the trees, wildflowers and various towns, I smiled and thought about my first educational experience. I began my education in a one-room school house with six classes; the first, second, third grades on one side, and the fourth, fifth, and sixth grades on the other. The Baptist church was next to the school. I had one teacher, Cousin Janie; I had to call her Mrs. Walker during class time. On Sundays, when she was my Sunday school teacher, I called her Cousin Janie.

Mrs. Walker had total control of her school house. She did not have an assistant principal or even a secretary. She was everything for that little school, from secretary to librarian, from administrator to teacher. I had so much respect for Mrs. Walker, and I thought that she knew everything. She taught me how to read using those little books that had one word on a page. Remember those little readers: *Spot. See Spot. See Spot run!* I thought that I was hot stuff because I could read the entire book. I loved school, and I knew that I was one of Mrs. Walker's favorite students. Even though she loved me, it was understood that, when some of the children reached a certain age, we were required to go to work in the cotton fields. My family was no exception. The other children remained in school.

Since I was the youngest of 11, when my turn came to report to the cotton fields, I was praying for a miracle. My siblings had told me such tall tales about the cotton fields, and I was afraid that I would not survive such hard work. However, off I went. I thought that I was going to die when I saw those long cotton rows. They extended as far as I could see. I felt as if I were drowning in an ocean of cotton. I put my sack on my back and began working my way down the rows. I could pick two rows at a time. As a matter of fact, I could pick a hundred pounds of cotton a day, which is a whole lot of cotton. My way of surviving the cotton fields was to sing. I always secretly wanted to be a singer or an actor. I remember sharing this ambition with my mother one day, and she told me to get a real job in education. Well, I was far from a teaching career at this point. I was in the middle of a cotton field, so I began to sing. I sounded so good to myself. I would sing all the way down the rows. By the time I looked up, I was at the end of my row, and the trees were giving me a standing ovation; they were applauding me! I bowed and said, "Thank you very much." I smiled and turned down the next rows.

Those were tough times, and it was even tougher when I returned to school, two months behind the other children. I was determined not only to catch up but to surpass my classmates. Some of the children would tease me because I was one of the cotton pickers. But every time I received a paper with an A on it, I would smile. My plan was working. I could beat them all in my studies. Therefore, I studied hard and learned my lessons. I was determined not to be beaten by my circumstances. I graduated co-salutatorian of my senior class.

In those days, flour was packaged in a large multicolor cloth sack. My parents could not afford to buy me nice clothes, so the flour sack served two purposes. Once my mother had used all of the flour baking for us, she would make my dresses from the flour sack material. I usually could see the same dress on Sundays at church on some of my little cousins, maybe made in a different style, but the same colors. I would smile, and I promised myself that one day I would own a silk dress or a nice suit.

Yes, I had a lot of time to think while riding on that Trailways bus until the driver announced that the next stop was Atlanta, Georgia. As I gathered up my luggage, a trunk and a suitcase, I was nervous and excited at the same time. When I got off the bus in downtown Atlanta, I wanted to appear sophisticated and not let anyone know that I was a small town country girl. I looked at all those taxis parked by the bus station, and with my $100 I began my journey in Atlanta. I had made it to my destination. Now what? I motioned for a taxi, as if I had done so a thousand times. My mother had told me to watch out for the city slickers, and I was not going to be taken. The taxi driver pulled up, and I told him to take me to the YWCA. Remember that my plan was to find a nice room at the YWCA. Out of all the taxi drivers in Atlanta, I had to pick the one who had never heard of the Y and had no idea where it was located. He drove around for what seemed like hours before he finally gave up. The poor man felt so bad that he did not even charge me a fare when he dropped me off downtown at the Marriott Courtyard on Courtland Street. With my $100, I checked in; it cost $20 a night. At this point, I was too tired to worry about it. When I checked into my room, I knew immediately that I had to come up with another plan. I remembered that my college classmate, John, had a sister who lived in Atlanta. I made contact with her, and she informed me that she knew a lady who rented rooms to college graduate students. I gave a sigh of relief. My plan was going to work after all.

Lois picked me up from the hotel early the next morning. She drove me to Mrs. Adams' house, rang the doorbell and left me there standing on the porch. Mrs. Adams lived near the West End, not too far from Atlanta University's campus. When Mrs. Adams came to the door, I explained to her that I had been accepted into graduate school, and I was there to rent one of her rooms. I could have fallen through her porch when she informed me that she did not rent her rooms to female students. She looked around to see that there was no one else there; I guess that she felt sorry for me. She told me that I could stay with her for one night. I thanked her and went inside as she showed me to my room. I quickly had to come up with another plan. I sat on my bed thinking about all of my choices. Is this the time to call home, call one of my brothers and sisters, and admit that I had made a mistake? All kinds of thoughts were going through my mind, but for tonight, I had a place to sleep. I would worry about tomorrow in the morning.

The next day, my plan was to find a job and another place to live. MARTA, the local bus line, cost fifteen cents one way. I boarded the bus to find a job in one day! I suddenly felt like a little country girl swallowed up by the big city. I went from one big building to another in downtown Atlanta that day searching for a job. I had taken typing and shorthand in high school, and I was praying that those skills would come in handy now. I walked and walked until I thought that my feet would fall off. Everybody in Atlanta had a college degree; every office was filled with applicants who looked so polished and sophisticated. Not only did I have to look for a job, I also had to get over to Atlanta University to secure funds for school. I did not have money to pay for the first class. I left the job search to go over to the campus to the financial aid office. Classes would begin the next day. I told the financial aid officer that I was there to attend school and that I needed loans to begin my classes. The lady looked at me as if I were crazy. However, she told me that she saw something in my face and that she was going to take a chance on me. She processed my paperwork, and I registered for three graduate courses. Even though I had other obstacles to overcome, I was in school. I smiled at that accomplishment and thanked God.

Atlanta University was not far from Paschal's Restaurant, and I went there to get something to eat. They had a job opening for a waitress at seventy-five cents an hour. I took the job. I finally made it back to Mrs. Adams' house late in the evening. I went straight to my room. She did not say anything, and neither did I. I kept waiting for her to come in and tell me that I had to leave. She never did. Each day, I went to class and work. We would speak to each other, and one day she invited me to eat her food. My waitress job lasted only one week. I was dismissed shortly after I accidentally poured water on a patron's expensive suit. I applied for an assistant teacher position with the Atlanta Public Schools, and I was hired. My one day with Mrs. Adams turned into nine months, and 30 years later, she calls me her daughter. I will forever be grateful to her for being my guardian angel. She provided the shelter that I needed to remain in Atlanta. She often teases me about finding me on her doorstep.

Success is truly a journey, and there will be plenty of obstacles and challenges to overcome, but there will also be angels and divine guidance to direct our paths. I was supposed to take every step that I took to reach where I am today: an author, an educator and a professional speaker. I became a full-time certified teacher with DeKalb County Public Schools, and I became a guidance counselor. I completed my graduate studies and I earned a Specialist degree in Guidance and Counseling. Back home, my former English teacher, Mrs. English (true name), mistakenly printed in the local paper that I had received my doctorate in Guidance and Counseling. She did not know that I had, at that time, earned only my Ed.S, a degree that comes after the Master's degree and before the doctorate. Well, that error prompted me to earn my doctorate in Counseling Psychology.

I think that it was prophetic; Mrs. English is 96-years-old, and she is still encouraging me. She keeps telling me that I will end up in the White House one day. We shall see.

Success is a journey, and each person has to find his or her own path. Determination was a key factor in my journey. Plus, I was hungry, figuratively and literally, to make it work. There were so many times when I wanted to give up and just go home, but something within gave me the strength to fight on. I know that it was my family, my faith and my belief in my God that sustained me. I quickly learned that everyone did not have the same visions that I had. Not intentionally to discourage me, but out of love, my sisters wanted me to come and live with them. They did not want to see me suffer; they were supportive. However, this was something new to our family, one of us going out on her own. I had to listen to the voice within. You will have to do the same thing. Follow your heart, be true to yourself and find your passion. The journey will not be easy, but it will be worth the ride. Avoid situations and people, including loved ones, who will try to discourage you. Set your course and stay with it. Even though there may be setbacks and obstacles to overcome, you, too, can smile through your storms.

Dr. Dovie Wesley Gray: is a retired educator/counselor for the DeKalb County School System, having served for over 27 years. She has been speaking professionally all over the country. Dr. Gray is an encourager, a motivator and an inspirational leader. Dr. Gray teaches graduate students in the Master's Degree Program at Capella University and Central Michigan University.

He Has Brought Me Too For to Leave Me Now
Joanne Jackson

"So we say with confidence, "The Lord is my Helper; I will not be afraid. What can man do to me?" ~ Hebrews 13:6.

As I look back over my life's journey, God has truly been good to me and my family, especially two of my grandchildren, Jasmine and Ebony. I want to take you back some 21 years to look at how God has ordered my steps.

I was a young bride and had a lot going for my family: a good husband and two wonderful girls. We had a beautiful home in a great neighborhood and a business that provided a profitable income. The girls went to the best of schools and really did not want for anything. My husband was very much involved in community affairs in our city. We had it going on.

Then something happened after 24 years of marriage. We decided to separate and divorced three years later. The oldest daughter was not married but the youngest was still at home. This separation was very hard on the younger child. She got involved with the wrong people and drugs came into play. Some time passed; she got married and had a baby. This child was in my care while my daughter dealt with her problems. Three years later, another child was born and again I had another baby to raise.

I spoke to God and told Him that if He made a way by providing for me and my grandchildren, I would raise them with no regrets, assured through my faith that God would be faithful and be my provider. I knew that this task was not going to be easy. The devil would always be present to discourage me and he was. He turned my daughter against me because she blamed me for her situation rather than accepting responsibility for her own actions. But through it all and what I was dealing with, I continued to pray for her.

Yes, the years were very hard. I had several jobs at the same time to make ends meet and to insure that my grandchildren received the best education. I denied myself any personal relationships so I could be available to meet their needs. I gave my total love to them. I would work from 8:00 a.m.to 4:00 p.m. with the school system and then work another job until 9:00 p.m. or later. My girl friends would pick up the girls from school and keep them going and keep the faith. We prayed a lot and had faith that God would turn things around for me.

I also had the responsibility of caring for my mother from 1985 until she passed in 1999. Before she went to be with the Lord, I took her to all the places she wanted to go: camping, Amtrak to ride the train to Santa Barbara, Oregon and many other places. The grand girls assisted me with her care and God will bless them for this. In June 1999, I retired after working 32 years so I could spend more quality time with my mother. In September 1999, my mother went to be with the Lord. In July 2000, my family moved from California to Georgia.

Both grandchildren graduated from high school and are attempting college. The oldest has one more year at Clark Atlanta University; the youngest is attending Georgia Perimeter College for two years and will transfer to Georgia State University in Atlanta, Georgia.

The girls' mother is doing great. She has turned her life over to God completely, and He has healed and released her from her addiction. She is married, has a good job and just brought a new home. My oldest daughter is a teacher and an ordained minister. She is getting her Master's in Theology.

God has ordered my steps throughout my journey. He never said it would be easy but He did say that He would never leave me. I don't regret all that I have been through because it has made me stronger in my faith and also a better person. One thing I know is that if you continue to pray and believe that God will change whatever situation is happening in you life, it will be so.

God has brought me too far to leave me. This is my assurance as I continue on my earthly journey.

Joanne Jackson is currently residing in Stone Mountain, Georgia. She is the proud mother of two wonderful daughters and grandmother of five beautiful children. She is a retired administrative assistant from the educational system of Oakland, California. She attends Victory Baptist Church in Stone Mountain, Georgia.

Angels Watching Over Me
Yvonne Givens

"Even though I walk through the valley of the shadow of death, I will fear no evil, for you are with me..." ~ Psalm 23:4

During those days I was always in a hurry. I was married and was a stay-at-home-mom. I had one child in high school, one in junior high and one in elementary school. Both our sons were in special programs which required me to alternate weeks with other moms in driving a car load of boys to school. In addition, I decided to return to school to obtain my Master's degree. Fortunately, my husband, Shelby, was very supportive.

He and I had decided to move from Sunnyvale, California to nearby Milpitas in order to allow our children to experience a truly multi-ethnic academic environment. We had a friend there who coordinated black history activities for African-American students and multicultural activities for the multi-ethnic school population. It was the perfect setting. This was quite a contrast from the predominantly white neighborhood schools in Sunnyvale.

The only drawback was that our daughter, Dianne, became a high school freshman before we moved. I circumvented the enrollment process by using the Milpitas address of a friend. This necessitated that I drive her to Milpitas High School (MHS) each

154

day in addition to chauffeuring the boys. She then could return home on public transportation. Mothers make great sacrifices for their children, often without their children realizing it.

It was an ordinary school day. I traveled the 30-mile trek without incident. I always avoided the congested streets leading directly to MHS by taking a less traveled route on Main Street.

I have no idea **how** my long, gold Chrysler station wagon made an unexpected sharp right turn near the end of that particular block. When I knew anything, half of my station wagon had jumped the curb, was up on the sidewalk, with the engine still running. I saw the fire hydrant out of my left window and a wire fence in front of me. Either I hit the brakes, or the car just stopped. I don't remember.

I did not hit the fire hydrant. I did not run into the fence. There was no walking pedestrian in sight. If there was a car behind me, it either stopped or went around me. Not one driver blew a horn. I was not physically hurt. My daughter, Dianne, was not injured. I was not frightened nor shaken up. And, there was no car damage.

I S-L-O-W-L-Y backed down and continued on my way to MHS. I then drove back 60 miles, passing my home in Milpitas, to Stanford University. I attended my classes for the day, went to the library to study, and returned home. The remainder of the day continued to be just ordinary. I greeted all three children as they returned from school, checked on their homework, prepared dinner, greeted Shelby when he came home from work and never spoke of the near - tragic event.

Years passed, and as I matured as a Christian, I realized how serious this accident had been and began to thank the Lord, profusely! **There must have been angels surrounding us inside the car, on the curb, on the sidewalk, in the street, in the air, and every other place possible!**

I thank God for His grace and mercy on that day for protecting my daughter and me, as well as others around us. PRAISE GOD FROM WHOM ALL BLESSINGS FLOW!

Yvonne Givens is currently living in Atlanta, Georgia. She matriculated through Teachers College in Chicago, Illinois. She taught many years in the Chicago and California School systems. She also was a curriculum specialist in the Christian academic setting at Green Pastures Christian Academy Schools in Decatur, Georgia. She has been a principal, church administrator and workshop presenter/lecturer. She is the mother of four children.

In Memory
We remember our Sisters On The Journey

Libby West - 2001
Founding Member and Visionary - 2001

Paulyne Depp – 2009
A quiet and loving spirit.

They have journeyed from earth to Glory.

We miss their love and presence.

They have left their footprints in the sand of
time as they soar to higher heights and now
rest in perfect peace with God.

Breinigsville, PA USA
03 November 2009
226949BV00001B/5/P

To learn more about WaterBrook Press and view
our catalog of products, log on to our Web site:

www.waterbrookpress.com

WATERBROOK
P R E S S